M000235657

Take
Our
Moments
and
Our Days

Take Our Moments and Our Days

AN ANABAPTIST PRAYER BOOK

Volume 1
ORDINARY TIME

Prepared by
Arthur Paul Boers ◆ Barbara Nelson Gingerich
Eleanor Kreider ◆ John Rempel ◆ Mary H. Schertz

Herald Press
Scottdale, Pennsylvania
Waterloo, Ontario

Library of Congress Cataloging-in-Publication Data
Boers, Arthur P. (Arthur Paul), 1957-
  Take our moments and our days : an anabaptist prayer book, ordi-
nary time / prepared by Arthur Paul Boers ... [et al.]. — [Rev. ed.]
    p. cm.
  Includes bibliographical references and index.
  ISBN 978-0-8361-9374-9 (hard cover: alk. paper)
  1. Mennonites—Prayers and devotions. 2. Morning prayer (Divine
office)—Mennonites—Texts. 3. Vespers—Mennonites—Texts. 4.
Anabaptists—Prayers and devotions. 5. Morning prayer (Divine
office)—Anabaptists—Texts. 6. Vespers—Anabaptists—Texts. 7.
Worship programs. I. Title.
  BX8125.B64 2007
  264'.09707—dc22

                              2007003667

Published in collaboration with Institute of Mennonite Studies,
Associated Mennonite Biblical Seminary, Elkhart, Indiana, USA

Unless otherwise indicated, Scripture readings are from the *New
Revised Standard Version Bible*, Copyright © 1989, by the Division of
Christian Education of the National Council of the Churches of Christ
in the USA, and are used by permission.

English translations of the Gloria Patri, the Benedictus, the Nunc
Dimittis, and the Magnificat © English Language Liturgical Consultation (ELLC), 1988, and used by permission. See: www.englishtexts.org

Psalms for each day are from *The Psalms: An Inclusive Language Version
Based on the Grail Translation from the Hebrew* (Chicago: GIA Publica-
tions, Inc., 2000). Copyright © 1963, 1986, 1993, 2000 The Grail (Eng-
land). GIA Publications, Inc., exclusive North American agent, 7404
S. Mason Ave., Chicago, IL 60638 www.gia music.com 800.442.1358
All rights reserved. Used by permission.

Reprinted by permission of HarperCollins Publishers Ltd. © The
Grail 1963, 1986, 1993, 1995.

TAKE OUR MOMENTS AND OUR DAYS
Copyright © 2007 by Herald Press, Scottdale, Pa. 15683
      Published simultaneously in Canada by Herald Press, Waterloo,
      Ont. N2L 6H7. All rights reserved
Library of Congress Catalog Card Number: 2007003667
International Standard Book Number: 978-0-8361-9374-9
Printed in Canada

Book design by Gwen Stamm; cover design by Merrill Miller

16 15 14 13 12 11 10   10 9 8 7 6 5 4 3 2

To order or request information, please call
1-800-245-7894, or visit www.heraldpress.com

We offer this prayer book
in the spirit of the compilers of the Ausbund,
a sixteenth-century Anabaptist hymnbook,
who dedicated their work
"in an unpartisan way"
for use by any and all Christians.

"Allen und jeden Christen
welcher Religion sie seyen,
unpartheyisch fast nützlich."

Contents

Preface

Recent years have seen the publication of many new prayer books. Do we need yet another? And why an Anabaptist-Mennonite one?

Although some Anabaptists centuries ago compiled prayer books, developing such resources now may seem a departure from our traditions and priorities. But we have discovered that many Mennonite pastors, church leaders, spiritual directors, scholars, and other believers are vitally interested in this form of prayer and now use prayer books from various sources. They are tapping into a time-honored practice of Christian daily prayer, and some are looking for resources that reflect the strengths of the radical reformation tradition. This growing Mennonite interest in morning and evening prayer practices provided the initial impetus for this project.

As we began posting on the Web site www.ambs.edu/prayerbook earlier drafts of the prayers collected in this volume, we were amazed and humbled to discover the extent of interest in Anabaptist-Mennonite prayer resources among Christians of other traditions. Repeatedly, we received messages from people of many denominations around the globe, expressing enthusiasm for the project and telling us about their experiences with this way of praying.

These grassroots users of earlier versions of the prayer book provided helpful insight into what worked well and what needed more refinement. We weighed carefully their thoughtful responses and reshaped these prayers accordingly. Most of all, respondents' words of appreciation provided much encouragement for our labors and sustained our sense that the project addresses a vital need.

We offer this volume of prayers for ordinary time as a gift to fellow Christians. Our desire is that use of these services will enrich the prayer of the church and its members. In the words of the old hymn, we pray that God will take our moments and our days and "let them flow in ceaseless praise."[1]

Finding biblical clues

The Psalms include frequent references to praying morning and evening. But the Psalmist does not intend that believers limit their praying to those times of day. Rather, praying at certain times fosters being prayerful all the time. Consider the repeated phrase in the first chapter of Genesis, "And there was evening and there was morning …" This shorthand denotes not just evening and morning but the passage of the whole day. In like manner, the Psalmist's

---

[1] "Take my life"; text by Frances R. Havergal, *Songs of Grace and Glory, Appendix,* 1874.

words, "From the rising of the sun to its setting the name of the LORD is to be praised" (Ps 113.3), indicate an aspiration to perpetual prayer.

Jesus made a similar recommendation. His parable about the persistent widow may puzzle us, but one point is plain: the story addresses his followers' need "to pray always and not to lose heart" (Lk 18.1).

The New Testament epistles pick up this theme. Paul urges believers to "rejoice always, pray without ceasing, give thanks in all circumstances" (1 Thess 5.16-18). We are told to "pray in the Spirit at all times" (Eph 6.18); "devote yourselves to prayer" (Col 4.2); "persevere in prayer" (Rom 12.12).

Praying without ceasing

The biblical counsel to "pray without ceasing" is clear, but how we do so is less apparent. A few believers have tried literally to live on prayer alone—without working, eating, sleeping—but Christian tradition sensibly cautions against such distortions. Christians today are more likely to say that our work or service is prayer. This approach to unceasing prayer may have more to commend it, but is it adequate? A few Christians live and work with steady awareness of God, but most of us need help to do so. Saying that everything we do is prayer may mean that in fact we rarely pray with conscious intention.

Our Sunday giving reminds us that all we have belongs to God; offerings make us mindful that all the ways we use money and other resources express our faith. In a similar way, morning and evening prayers remind us that all our time belongs to God. Morning and evening prayer is not about praying only at those times of day, any more than tithing is about granting God's ownership of just ten percent of our money.

Morning and evening symbolize all time. They are key daily moments when we set our direction, remember our purpose, review how God is at work, and recall where we missed God's priorities. Regular, disciplined prayers at particular times encourage us to be prayerful always.

Supporting one another in prayer

Many Christians struggle with prayer. We may not know how or when to pray, what to say, how to start, or when we are finished. Some have never settled into habits of prayer. Others have ceased to pray for a variety of reasons. Because challenges of busyness are pressing spiritual issues today, we may have trouble finding time for prayer. Patterned prayer helps many of us pray—or pray again. Some who learn this way of praying report, "Until now I was not able to pray."

Prayer books can give us the encouragement of praying with others. Here as elsewhere, we experience the truth of the Anabaptist conviction that we need the body of Christ. Given our society's individualism, we may tend to think it noble for each person always to pray freely, spontaneously, alone, one's own way, according to one's own inspirations. But the current narrow emphasis on private prayer was not characteristic of Bible times or of the church in the early centuries. And the truth is, constancy in prayer—like all faithful living—typically relies on the help and support of other believers.

Morning and evening prayer touches on issues that run throughout Christian history: the relationship of individual and corporate prayer, unplanned and set prayers, fixed-time and unceasing prayer. All have value, not as ends in themselves but to the extent that they lead us to God. Our hope is that through these morning and evening prayers, believers may experience the truth of the Psalmist's words of praise: "You make the gateways of the morning and the evening shout for joy" (Ps 65.8).

Acknowledgments

From its inception, this project has relied on the generous contributions of many, and our circle of benefactors continues to expand.

A group of North American Mennonite leaders came together, initially to dream about the project and later to evaluate what we learned from response to the first two draft versions of *Take Our Moments and Our Days*. J. Nelson Kraybill, then president of Associated Mennonite Biblical Seminary (AMBS), enthusiastically supported this venture and helped fund that early consultation through the Presidential Vision Fund. From then on, our work was generously underwritten by The Anabaptist Foundation, Vancouver, BC, and its president, J. Evan Kreider.

The Institute of Mennonite Studies at AMBS endorsed the project and made staff time available to help bring it to fruition. From her expertise in church music, Associate Professor of Worship and the Arts Rebecca Slough proposed a wealth of song selections. Out of his deep love and vast knowledge of scripture, Professor Emeritus of New Testament Willard M. Swartley aided our committee with a final round of text selections. With her customary skill and grace, Director of Communications Mary E. Klassen has provided invaluable help with publicity and maintenance of the prayer book Web pages.

Mennonite Church USA and Mennonite Church Canada created Web links to previous versions of the prayers, which helped connect us with believers in far-flung places. The responses of these users have assisted and encouraged our work in more ways than we can say.

Prayerful poets enriched the services by composing collects to complete each day's intercessory prayer. Our thanks to Gayle Gerber Koontz for morning and evening collects for Week 1, Andrew Kreider for Week 2, Lois Siemens for Week 3, and Darrin Snyder Belousek for Week 4.

Tireless and multitalented volunteer James Nelson Gingerich formatted the book. He has also provided critical assistance to the project by refining and maintaining our scripture selection database, begun through the efforts of AMBS student Christine Guth.

We are grateful for the AMBS community that has nurtured this project, for its prayerful engagement with scripture, which seeks to form lives suited to witness to God's extravagant and costly love for the world.

And we thank God for colleagues whose good humor, varied abilities—as liturgists, theologians, scripture scholars, editors—and common passion for prayer have made collaborating on this project a source of so much satisfaction and joy.

Introduction

A threefold pattern of praising, listening, and
responding is how Christians pray. We honor
God and give thanks. Then we listen to God
through Bible readings, in quiet moments of
intentional waiting for God's voice, or sometimes through other people's words. And finally
we respond to God, giving the love of our
hearts and the renewed dedication of our lives,
interceding for others, and receiving a blessing.
Whether we are young or old, in families or as
individuals, accustomed to formal prayers or
spontaneous ones, Christians naturally pray in
this three-part form. *Take Our Moments and Our
Days* reflects this familiar way of praying.

Scripture-saturated prayer

The words of these prayers are taken directly
from the Bible or use words minimally adapted
from it.[1] In each service we read a psalm portion,
a Gospel text, and another scripture passage.
The structure of the services, the three calls—to
praise, discipleship, and intercession—use scripture words, as do the words of thanksgiving

---

1 See indexes for a list of all scripture references. Bible
readings are from the New Revised Standard Version;
Psalm portions use *The Psalms: An Inclusive Language Version
Based on the Grail Translation from the Hebrew* (Chicago: GIA
Publications, Inc., 2000). Where it is different from the Grail's,
NRSV versification appears in brackets.

and (in the evening) confession. Every service includes a Gospel song—of Zechariah, Mary, or Simeon—or a recitation of the Beatitudes. In each service we pray the Lord's Prayer and hear a biblical benediction.

Early Anabaptists learned much scripture by heart; we hope that those who use these services will be inspired to do the same. We trust that by praying these scripture-saturated prayers, you will find your days and nights suffused with "the remembered Word," a hallmark of Anabaptist spirituality.

Anabaptist coloration

The prominent place given to Jesus in these prayers also resonates with a sixteenth-century Anabaptist concern: following Christ in life. The themes chosen for these prayers for ordinary time are important elements in the New Testament witness to Jesus: the Lord's Prayer (the focus of Week 1), the Beatitudes (Week 2), the parables of Jesus (Week 3), and the signs and wonders performed by Jesus (Week 4). The focus on Jesus' life and teachings in these services is intended to aid us in deeply internalizing Jesus' example and his words of challenge and comfort.

The scriptures selected reflect intensive work by the editorial committee to identify foundational texts of early Anabaptists. Selections also speak to concerns of Anabaptists today, such as peace, justice, ecology, feminist sensitivities, ecumenical commitments, and regard for each testament, in its own right, as God's inspired word.

Notes on using
Take Our Moments and Our Days

Try to set a regular time for prayer. Few of us find time for sustained prayer both morning and evening, so adopt either pattern. If possible, create a physical setting conducive to praying. You might want to have a visual focus—an open Bible, a cross, candle, symbol, or picture.

If you are praying in a group, any designated person can lead the services. Leader parts are in regular type; others present respond by reading the bold italic type. If a scripture text is very brief, reading it a second time may help you memorize it.

An overarching scripture text for each week provides title lines and opening sentences and sets the tone for the week's thematically linked Bible readings. Organizing texts for the four weeks are the Lord's Prayer, Matthew 6.9-13 Week 1); the Beatitudes, Matthew 5.3-12 (Week 2); Psalm 78.1-7 (Week 3); and Luke 4.17-19 (Week 4).

The services have a simple three-part form—praise, listen, respond—which is evident in the three calls: call to praise, call to discipleship, call to intercession. Proceed through these parts at an unhurried pace that allows ample time—breathing space—for meditation.

James E. Clemens has composed lovely musical settings for some repeated parts of the services. Note that one set (pages 403–6) is for unison singing (with guitar chords); the other (pages 407–11) is for singing in parts.

Call to praise

The first section of each service features praise of God through psalm prayer, personal thanksgiving, and song.

After the call to praise, the word "Glory ..." signals a traditional Christian outburst of praise directed toward God. We provide two forms of this doxology on page 11 or invite you to use another expression of praise. Several sung and spoken doxologies are also listed there.

The psalm may be prayed in alternating voices (leader and congregation, or responsively by two parts of the gathered group) as indicated with regular and bold italic type.

Verses from the Psalms frame open space for brief spontaneous prayers of thanksgiving.

Songs in the first section address God with our praise and thanksgiving. Numbers listed refer to songs in these resources: *Hymnal: A Worship Book* (Scottdale, PA: Mennonite Publishing House, 1992); *Sing the Journey* (Scottdale, PA: Faith & Life Resources, 2005); and *Sing the Story* (Scottdale, PA: Faith & Life Resources, 2007). Many of these hymns appear in other hymnals. You may substitute or add songs from other sources. Some people enjoy reading hymn texts as devotional poetry instead of singing them. Note that a list of other suitable songs appears as an appendix to this book.

In the evening the first section ends with verses from Psalm 51, which surround moments of silent confession.

Call to discipleship

The second section is a call to listen to the voice of Jesus, and to express our desire to follow in his way.

The Great Commandment (every morning) and the bread of life words (every evening) anchor us to the heart of Jesus' vocation and message.

Gospel readings follow the week's theme as indicated in the opening sentences of each service. The second Bible reading coordinates with the Gospel reading of the day and may be drawn from either the Old or the New Testament. You may wish to omit, substitute, or add a reading.

During the brief reflection on the readings, you may pause in silence, simply repeat a word or phrase from the reading, or comment on a connection between the readings or with events of the day. This is not a time for discussion but rather for heartfelt response to the readings. Anabaptist tradition is characterized by a conviction that the Spirit may illumine scripture through any participant's comment.

The songs listed after the readings reflect the day's theme and provide opportunity to respond in gratitude, affirmation of faith, and self-dedication. Again, the hymn texts may be sung or spoken. Consult the appendix for more song selections.

Zechariah's song, Mary's song, and Simeon's song are canticles (biblical songs) traditionally associated with morning and evening prayers. The texts for these songs are printed on pages 12 to 16. In Week 2, recitation of the Beatitudes (page 17) takes the place of a canticle. Our hope is that frequent repetition of these vital texts will help you learn them by heart, in all the rich meanings of that phrase.

Call to intercession

In the third section, we continue to respond to the reading of scripture by praying for ourselves and those dear to us, for our community, for the church, for the world, and for other concerns we carry. Using words of scripture, we are called (mornings) to unworried, loving prayers and (evenings) to thankful and confident intercession.

As each of the five subjects for intercession is introduced, allow plenty of opportunity for open, free prayers before concluding with the simple responsive phrase provided. Morning and evening intercessions will be the same on any given day, and their imagery is drawn from the morning and evening readings for the day. Note that the petitions for the church and the world change each day throughout the week. If you use only one service for a particular day, notice the content of these intercessions on the other days; you may want to combine or adapt the materials to suit your occasion.

A brief prayer (loosely following the traditional form known as a "collect") draws the intercessions to a close and creates a bridge to the Lord's Prayer. Three forms of the Lord's Prayer are printed on pages 18 and 19.

The benedictions are all scriptural. Some groups conclude their prayer service with a period of silence, a simple song of peace and blessing, or by extending the peace of Christ to one another.

Flexible adaptation of the services

However you adapt the services, keep the threefold structure—praise, listen, respond—clear.

You may use these materials to lead public worship. Adapt them by adding spontaneous elements, songs, longer Bible readings,[1] meditation on the readings, readings by spiritual writ-

---

[1] On occasion, suggested longer readings are indicated by the verses in parentheses.

ers, more silence, additional canticles, a sermon, testimony, or free prayers.

You may shorten the services as well. For example, you may memorize the three calls and pray them by heart amid the activities of your day. Then add your personal petitions and finish by praying the Lord's Prayer.

If you are not used to reading written prayers, you may still find something of value here. In each service, you will find Psalm verses and words or stories of Jesus which can provide a setting for your informal prayers. After reading the Bible passages, you can put the book aside and pray freely. You may wish to return for the blessing.

The services are suited to group or individual prayers. Even when you pray alone, you know that your prayers join the prayers of many others.

Other resources

A second volume, of morning and evening prayers for the seasons of the Christian year, from Advent through Pentecost, is also available from Herald Press. For more information and other prayer resources see http://www.mpn. net/takeourmoments. Especially illuminating as background for using *Take Our Moments and Our Days: An Anabaptist Prayer Book* is a scholarly but accessible study of Anabaptist spirituality by C. Arnold Snyder: *Following in the Footsteps of Christ: The Anabaptist Tradition* (Maryknoll, NY: Orbis Books, 2004).

A recently revised and expanded book by Arthur Paul Boers, *Day by Day These Things We Pray: Uncovering Ancient Rhythms of Prayer* (Scottdale, PA: Herald Press, 2010), is a thoughtful and accessible introduction to the practice of daily prayer and a good guide for those wondering about or eager to begin the spiritual journey of corporate praying. It includes a useful list of resources, along with suggestions for preparing a prayer space and enriching your practice of prayer.

Repeated elements

Glory …

Glory to the Father,
and to the Son,
and to the Holy Spirit:
as it was in the beginning,
is now,
and will be for ever. Amen.[1]

Praise God …

Praise God, the Abba bearing love;
Praise God, the Servant from above;
Praise God, the Paraclete we share:
O triune God, receive our prayer.[2]

Sung doxologies[3]

Praise God, the Source of life (H95)
Praise God from whom (H118, H119)
To God, with the Lamb (H125)
Glory be to the Father (H127)

---

[1] This translation of the Gloria Patri was prepared by the English Language Liturgical Consultation (ELLC), 1988.

[2] Gail Ramshaw-Schmidt, "Naming the Trinity: Orthodoxy and Inclusivity," *Worship* 60, no. 6 (November 1986): 497–98.

[3] Numbers refer to *Hymnal: A Worship Book* (Scottdale, PA: Mennonite Publishing House, 1992). Many hymns end with a doxological verse; see, for example, the final verses of the following: 22, 48, 52, 85, 86, 121, 177, 179, 183, 236, 256, 264, 441, 492, 650, 658.

Zechariah's song

Blessed be the Lord, the God of Israel,
who has come to his people and set them free.
The Lord has raised up for us a mighty Savior,
born of the house of his servant David.
Through the holy prophets, God promised of old
to save us from our enemies,
from the hands of all who hate us,
to show mercy to our forebears,
and to remember his holy covenant.
This was the oath God swore
     to our father Abraham:
to set us free from the hands of our enemies,
free to worship him without fear,
holy and righteous before him,
all the days of our life.

And you, child, shall be called
     the prophet of the Most High,
for you will go before the Lord to prepare his way,
to give his people knowledge of salvation
by the forgiveness of their sins.
In the tender compassion of our God
the dawn from on high shall break upon us,
to shine on those who dwell in darkness
     and the shadow of death,
and to guide our feet into the way of peace.[4]

---

[4] This translation of Luke 1:68-79 was prepared by the English Language Liturgical Consultation (ELLC), 1988.

Zechariah's song

Blessed are you, Lord, the God of Israel,
you have come to your people and set them free.
You have raised up for us a mighty Savior,
born of the house of your servant David.
Through your holy prophets, you promised of old
to save us from our enemies,
from the hands of all who hate us,
to show mercy to our forebears,
and to remember your holy covenant.
This was the oath you swore
  to our father Abraham:
to set us free from the hands of our enemies,
free to worship you without fear,
holy and righteous before you,
all the days of our life.

And you, child, shall be called the prophet
  of the Most High,
for you will go before the Lord to prepare the way,
to give God's people knowledge of salvation
by the forgiveness of their sins.
In the tender compassion of our God
the dawn from on high shall break upon us,
to shine on those who dwell in darkness
  and the shadow of death,
and to guide our feet into the way of peace.[5]

---

[5] This alternative version of Luke 1:68-79 was prepared by
the English Language Liturgical Consultation (ELLC), 1988.

Sung settings of Zechariah's song

Bless'd be the God of Israel (H174)
Blessed be the Lord (H179)

Simeon's song

Now, Lord, you let your servant go in peace:
your word has been fulfilled.
My own eyes have seen the salvation
which you have prepared
*   in the sight of every people:*
a light to reveal you to the nations
and the glory of your people Israel.[6]

Sung settings of Simeon's song

Lord, bid your servant go (H179, accompaniment
   book)

Spoken setting of Simeon's song

NRSV version (H771)

---

[6] This translation of Luke 2.29-32 was prepared by the
English Language Liturgical Consultation (ELLC), 1988.

Mary's song

My soul proclaims the greatness of the Lord,
my spirit rejoices in God my Savior,
who has looked with favor
   on his lowly servant.
From this day
   all generations will call me blessed:
the Almighty has done great things for me
and holy is his name.
God has mercy on those who fear him,
from generation to generation.
The Lord has shown strength with his arm
and scattered the proud in their conceit,
casting down the mighty from their thrones
and lifting up the lowly.
God has filled the hungry with good things
and sent the rich away empty.
He has come to the aid of his servant Israel,
to remember the promise of mercy,
the promise made to our forebears,
to Abraham and his children for ever.[7]

Spoken settings for responsive reading

An ELLC version (H840)
A version using direct address to God (H715)

---

[7] This translation of Luke 1:46-55 was prepared by the
English Language Liturgical Consultation (ELLC), 1988.

Mary's song

My soul proclaims the greatness of the Lord,
my spirit rejoices in God my Savior,
for you, Lord, have looked with favor
   on your lowly servant.
From this day
   all generations will call me blessed:
you, the Almighty, have done great things for me
and holy is your name.
You have mercy on those who fear you,
from generation to generation.
You have shown strength with your arm
and scattered the proud in their conceit,
casting down the mighty from their thrones
and lifting up the lowly.
You have filled the hungry with good things
and sent the rich away empty.
You have come to the aid
   of your servant Israel,
to remember the promise of mercy,
the promise made to our forebears,
to Abraham and his children for ever.[8]

Sung settings of Mary's song

My soul proclaims with wonder (H181)
My soul is filled with joy (SJ13)

---

[8] This alternative version of Luke 1:46-55 was prepared by
the English Language Liturgical Consultation (ELLC), 1988.

The Beatitudes

Blessed are the poor in spirit,
for theirs is the kingdom of heaven.
Blessed are those who mourn,
for they will be comforted.
Blessed are the meek,
for they will inherit the earth.
Blessed are those who hunger and thirst
for righteousness, for they will be filled.
Blessed are the merciful,
for they will receive mercy.
Blessed are the pure in heart,
for they will see God.
Blessed are the peacemakers,
for they will be called children of God.
Blessed are those who are persecuted
for righteousness' sake,
for theirs is the kingdom of heaven.
Blessed are you when people revile you
and persecute you
and utter all kinds of evil against you falsely
on my account.
Rejoice and be glad,
for your reward is great in heaven,
for in the same way
they persecuted the prophets
who were before you.[9]

---

[9] Matthew 5.3-12.

Our Father in heaven

Our Father in heaven,
hallowed be your name,
your kingdom come,
your will be done,
on earth as in heaven.
Give us today our daily bread.
Forgive us our sins
as we forgive those who sin against us.
Save us from the time of trial
and deliver us from evil.

For the kingdom, the power, and the glory
   are yours
now and forever. Amen.[10]

Sung settings of the Lord's Prayer

Our Father, which art in heaven (SJ48)
Our Father who art in heaven (H228)
Our Father who art in heaven (H351)
Our Father who art in heaven (H554, with
   verses)

Spoken settings of the Lord's Prayer

The ELLC version (H731)

---

[10]   This translation of the Lord's Prayer was prepared
by the English Language Liturgical Consultation (ELLC),
1988.

Our Father who art in heaven

Our Father who art in heaven,
hallowed be thy name.
Thy kingdom come, thy will be done
on earth as it is in heaven.
Give us this day our daily bread,
and forgive us our debts,
as we forgive our debtors.
And lead us not into temptation,
but deliver us from evil,
for thine is the kingdom, and the power,
and the glory forever. Amen.

Our Father in heaven

Our Father in heaven,
hallowed be your name.
Your kingdom come.
Your will be done, on earth as it is in heaven.
Give us this day our daily bread.
And forgive us our debts,
as we also have forgiven our debtors.
And do not bring us to the time of trial,
but rescue us from the evil one.[11]

---

[11] Matthew 6.9-13.

WEEK 1

Lord's Prayer

Our Father in heaven

Opening sentence
Our Father in heaven,
hallowed be your name.

Call to praise

Lord, open our lips
and our mouths will proclaim your praise.
You are good to those who wait for you,
to all who seek you.

Glory ...

Psalm 104.1-4, 10-15
Bless the LORD, my soul!
LORD God, how great you are,
clothed in majesty and glory,
wrapped in light as in a robe!

You stretch out the heavens like a tent.
Above the rains you build your dwelling.
You make the clouds your chariot,
you walk on the wings of the wind;
you make the winds your messengers
and flashing fire your servants.

You make springs gush forth in the valleys;
they flow in between the hills.
They give drink to all the beasts of the field;
the wild asses quench their thirst.
On their banks dwell the birds of heaven;
from the branches they sing their song.

From your dwelling you water the hills;
earth drinks its fill of your gift.
You make the grass grow for the cattle
and the plants to serve our needs,

that we may bring forth bread from the earth
and wine to cheer our hearts;
oil, to make our faces shine
and bread to strengthen our hearts.

Thanksgiving

My heart is ready, O God;
I will sing your praise.
Your steadfast love is higher than the heavens,
and your faithfulness reaches to the clouds.
(free prayers of thanksgiving)
Be exalted, O God, above the heavens,
and let your glory shine over all the earth.
Amen.

Song

O day of rest and gladness (H641)
Praise the Lord, sing hallelujah (H50)
From the hands (H97)

Call to discipleship

Jesus said, Let anyone with ears to hear listen.
You shall love the Lord your God
with all your heart, and with all your soul,
and with all your strength,
and with all your mind;
and your neighbor as yourself.
Do this, and you will live.
Lord Jesus, you have the words of eternal life.

Luke 11.1-4, (5-8), 9-13

[Jesus] was praying in a certain place, and after he had finished, one of his disciples said to him, "Lord, teach us to pray, as John taught his disciples." He said to them, "When you pray, say:

Father, hallowed be your name.
Your kingdom come.
Give us each day our daily bread.
And forgive us our sins,
for we ourselves forgive everyone indebted to us.
And do not bring us to the time of trial."

…"So I say to you, Ask, and it will be given you; search, and you will find; knock, and the door will be opened for you. For everyone who asks receives, and everyone who searches finds, and for everyone who knocks, the door will be opened. Is there anyone among you who, if your child asks for a fish, will give a snake instead of a fish? Or if the child asks for an egg, will give a scorpion? If you then, who are evil, know how to give good gifts to your children, how much more will the heavenly Father give the Holy Spirit to those who ask him!"

Ephesians 3.14-19

For this reason I bow my knees before the Father, from whom every family in heaven and on earth takes its name. I pray that, according to the riches of his glory, he may grant that you may be strengthened in your inner being with power through his Spirit, and that Christ may dwell in your hearts through faith, as you are being rooted and grounded in love. I pray that you may have the power to comprehend, with all the saints, what is the breadth and length and height and depth, and to know the love of Christ that surpasses knowledge, so that you may be filled with all the fullness of God.

Silent or spoken reflection on the readings

Song

Our Father, which art in heaven (SJ48)

Lord, teach us how to pray aright (H350)
Love divine, all loves excelling (H592)

Zechariah's song

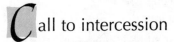

all to intercession

Rejoice in the Lord always.
The Lord is near.
Do not worry about anything,
but in everything with thanksgiving
let your requests be made known to God.

Holy God, we bring our prayers to you as acts
of love for you and for our neighbors.
In your mercy, Lord, hear our prayer.

You give us bread to strengthen our hearts.
We pray for ourselves and those dear to us.
(open prayers)
Our Father in heaven,
hallowed be your name.

Your love knows no partiality. We pray for our
community and for our neighbors.
(open prayers)
Our Father in heaven,
hallowed be your name.

You fill your people with the love of Christ.
We pray for the church in all places, that we
may be one.
(open prayers)
Our Father in heaven,
hallowed be your name.

You are the Lord of all you have made. We
pray for the world, that your reign may come
and your will be done on earth.
(open prayers)
Our Father in heaven,
hallowed be your name.

We offer you other concerns we carry in our
hearts.
(open prayers)
Our Father in heaven,
hallowed be your name.

God of grace and glory,
you fling the stars into the heavens;
you see every sparrow fall.
Deepen our trust in the mystery
of your power shining through Christ Jesus,
that we may live your love for the world.
In the name of the one
who taught us we pray:

Our Father ...

Benediction

May the grace of the Lord Jesus Christ,
the love of God,
and the communion of the Holy Spirit
be with us. Amen.

Hallowed be your name

Opening sentence

Our Father in heaven,
hallowed be your name.

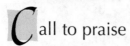 **all to praise**

O God, your word is a lamp to my feet
and a light to my path.
The light and peace of Jesus Christ be with us.

Glory ...

Psalm 103.1-7

My soul, give thanks to the LORD,
all my being, bless God's holy name.
My soul, give thanks to the LORD
and never forget all God's blessings.

It is God who forgives all your guilt,
who heals every one of your ills,
who redeems your life from the grave,
who crowns you with love and compassion,
who fills your life with good things,
renewing your youth like an eagle's.

The LORD does deeds of justice,
gives judgment for all who are oppressed.

The Lord's ways were made known to Moses;
the Lord's deeds to Israel's children.

Thanksgiving

It is good to give thanks to the Lord,
to sing praises to your name, O Most High.
(free prayers of thanksgiving)
We declare your steadfast love in the morning,
and your faithfulness by night. Amen.

Song

The day you gave us, Lord (H652)
Heilig, heilig, heilig (Holy, holy, holy) (H75)
Holy God, we praise thy name (H121)

Confession

Have mercy on me, O God,
according to your steadfast love;
according to your abundant mercy
blot out my transgressions.
(silence)
Create in me a clean heart, O God,
and put a new and right spirit within me.
Restore to me the joy of your salvation
and sustain in me a willing spirit. Amen.

Call to discipleship

Jesus said, I am the bread of life.
Whoever comes to me will never be hungry,

and whoever believes in me
will never be thirsty.
Lord Jesus, you have the words of eternal life.

John 20.11-18

But Mary stood weeping outside the tomb.
As she wept, she bent over to look into the
tomb; and she saw two angels in white, sitting where the body of Jesus had been lying,
one at the head and the other at the feet. They
said to her, "Woman, why are you weeping?"
She said to them, "They have taken away my
Lord, and I do not know where they have
laid him." When she had said this, she turned
around and saw Jesus standing there, but she
did not know that it was Jesus. Jesus said to
her, "Woman, why are you weeping? Whom
are you looking for?" Supposing him to be
the gardener, she said to him, "Sir, if you have
carried him away, tell me where you have
laid him, and I will take him away." Jesus
said to her, "Mary!" She turned and said to
him in Hebrew, "Rabbouni!" (which means
Teacher). Jesus said to her, "Do not hold on
to me, because I have not yet ascended to the
Father. But go to my brothers and say to them,
'I am ascending to my Father and your Father,
to my God and your God.'" Mary Magdalene
went and announced to the disciples, "I have

seen the Lord"; and she told them that he had
said these things to her.

Ephesians 4.4-6

There is one body and one Spirit, just as you
were called to the one hope of your calling,
one Lord, one faith, one baptism, one God and
Father of all, who is above all and through all
and in all.

Silent or spoken reflection on the readings

Song

Our Father who art in heaven (H228)
One is the body (SJ72)
Christ is alive! Let Christians sing (H278)

Mary's *or* Simeon's song

Call to intercession

Ask, and it will be given you;
search, and you will find;
knock, and the door will be opened for you.
*The heavenly Father will give the Holy Spirit
to those who ask.*

Holy God, we bring our prayers to you with
confidence, in the name of our Lord Jesus.
In your mercy, Lord, hear our prayer.

You give us bread to strengthen our hearts.
We pray for ourselves and those dear to us.
(open prayers)
Our Father in heaven,
hallowed be your name.

Your love knows no partiality. We pray for our
community and for our neighbors.
(open prayers)
Our Father in heaven,
hallowed be your name.

You fill your people with the love of Christ.
We pray for the church in all places, that we
may be one.
(open prayers)
Our Father in heaven,
hallowed be your name.

You are the Lord of all you have made. We
pray for the world, that your reign may come
and your will be done on earth.
(open prayers)
Our Father in heaven,
hallowed be your name.

We offer you other concerns we carry in our
hearts.
(open prayers)
Our Father in heaven,
hallowed be your name.

God of grace and glory,
you keep our souls,
satisfying us with living bread and holy work.
Renew us through forgiveness
and restore us in rest,
that we may look for the coming of your reign
on earth as in heaven.
Secure in your love,
we pray with humility and joy:

Our Father ...

Benediction

May the grace of the Lord Jesus Christ,
the love of God,
and the communion of the Holy Spirit
be with us. Amen.

Your kingdom come

Opening sentences
Your kingdom come.
Your will be done on earth as in heaven.

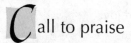all to praise

Lord, open our lips
and our mouths will proclaim your praise.
You are good to those who wait for you,
to all who seek you.

Glory ...

Psalm 99.1-5
The LORD is king; the peoples tremble.
He is throned on the cherubim;
   the earth quakes.
The LORD is great in Zion;

You are supreme over all the peoples.
Let them praise your name,
  so terrible and great,
so holy, full of power.

You are a king who loves what is right;
you have established equity, justice and right;
you have established them in Jacob.

Exalt the LORD our God;
bow down before God's footstool.
The LORD our God is holy.

Thanksgiving

My heart is ready, O God;
I will sing your praise.
Your steadfast love is higher than the heavens,
and your faithfulness reaches to the clouds.
(free prayers of thanksgiving)
Be exalted, O God, above the heavens,
and let your glory shine over all the earth.
Amen.

Song

Jubilate Deo omnis terra (H103)
All people that on earth do dwell (H42)
Praise with joy the world's Creator (SJ16)

Call to discipleship

Jesus said, Let anyone with ears to hear listen.
You shall love the Lord your God
with all your heart, and with all your soul,
and with all your strength,
and with all your mind;
and your neighbor as yourself.
Do this, and you will live.
Lord Jesus, you have the words of eternal life.

Luke 17.20-21

Once Jesus was asked by the Pharisees when the kingdom of God was coming, and he answered, "The kingdom of God is not coming with things that can be observed; nor will they say, 'Look, here it is!' or 'There it is!' For, in fact, the kingdom of God is among you."

Romans 14.15-17

If your brother or sister is being injured by what you eat, you are no longer walking in love. Do not let what you eat cause the ruin of one for whom Christ died. So do not let your good be spoken of as evil. For the kingdom of God is not food and drink but righteousness and peace and joy in the Holy Spirit.

Silent or spoken reflection on the readings

Song

Mayenziwe (Your will be done) (SJ57)
Christ, from whom all blessings (H365)
Heart with loving heart united (H420)

Zechariah's song

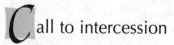

Call to intercession

Rejoice in the Lord always.
The Lord is near.

Do not worry about anything,
but in everything with thanksgiving
let your requests be made known to God.

Abba God, we bring our prayers to you as
acts of love for you and for our neighbors.
In your mercy, Lord, hear our prayer.

Your presence and your reign are already with
us. We pray for ourselves and those dear to us.
(open prayers)
Your kingdom come,
your will be done on earth as in heaven.

Your faithfulness lasts forever. We pray for
our community and for our neighbors.
(open prayers)
Your kingdom come,
your will be done on earth as in heaven.

Your people serve you with gladness. We pray
for the church in all places, that we may know
the freedom of life in the Spirit.
(open prayers)
Your kingdom come,
your will be done on earth as in heaven.

Your way is justice and peace. We pray for the
world and for all who care for creation.
(open prayers)
Your kingdom come,
your will be done on earth as in heaven.

We offer you other concerns we carry in our hearts.
(open prayers)
Your kingdom come,
your will be done on earth as in heaven.

God of grace and glory,
you fling the stars into the heavens;
you see every sparrow fall.
Deepen our trust in the mystery
of your power shining through Christ Jesus,
that we may live your love for the world.
In the name of the one
who taught us we pray:

Our Father ...

Benediction
May the God of hope
fill us with all joy and peace in believing
so that we may abound in hope
by the power of the Holy Spirit. Amen.

On earth as in heaven

Opening sentences

Your kingdom come.
Your will be done on earth as in heaven.

Call to praise

O God, your word is a lamp to my feet
and a light to my path.
The light and peace of Jesus Christ be with us.

Glory ...

Psalm 103.19-22

The LORD has set his throne in heaven
and his kingdom rules over all.
Give thanks to the LORD, all you angels,
mighty in power, fulfilling God's word,
who heed the voice of that word.

Give thanks to the LORD, all you hosts,
you servants who do God's will.
Give thanks to the LORD, all his works,
in every place where God rules.
My soul, give thanks to the LORD!

Thanksgiving

It is good to give thanks to the Lord,
to sing praises to your name, O Most High.
(free prayers of thanksgiving)
We declare your steadfast love in the morning,
and your faithfulness by night. Amen.

Song

For God so loved us (H167)
I'll praise my Maker (H166)
Cantai ao Senhor (O sing to the Lord) (SJ12)

Confession

Have mercy on me, O God,
according to your steadfast love;
according to your abundant mercy
blot out my transgressions.
(silence)
Create in me a clean heart, O God,
and put a new and right spirit within me.
Restore to me the joy of your salvation
and sustain in me a willing spirit. Amen.

Call to discipleship

Jesus said, I am the bread of life.
Whoever comes to me will never be hungry,
and whoever believes in me
will never be thirsty.
Lord Jesus, you have the words of eternal life.

Luke 10.5-11

"Whatever house you enter, first say, 'Peace to this house!' And if anyone is there who shares in peace, your peace will rest on that person; but if not, it will return to you. Remain in the same house, eating and drinking whatever they provide, for the laborer deserves to be paid. Do not move about from house to house. Whenever you enter a town and its people welcome you, eat what is set before you; cure the sick who are there, and say to them, 'The kingdom of God has come near to you.' But whenever you enter a town and they do not welcome you, go out into its streets and say, 'Even the dust of your town that clings to our feet, we wipe off in protest against you. Yet know this: the kingdom of God has come near.'"

Revelation 21.1-4

Then I saw a new heaven and a new earth; for the first heaven and the first earth had passed away, and the sea was no more. And I saw the holy city, the new Jerusalem, coming down out of heaven from God, prepared as a bride adorned for her husband. And I heard a loud voice from the throne saying,

"See, the home of God is among mortals.
He will dwell with them as their God;
they will be his peoples,

and God himself will be with them;
he will wipe every tear from their eyes.
Death will be no more;
mourning and crying and pain will be no
    more,
for the first things have passed away."

Silent or spoken reflection on the readings

Song
New earth, heavens new (H299)
Oh, holy city seen of John (H320)
Joy to the world (H318)

Mary's *or* Simeon's song

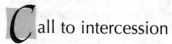

*C*all to intercession

Ask, and it will be given you;
search, and you will find;
knock, and the door will be opened for you.
***The heavenly Father will give the Holy Spirit
to those who ask.***

Abba God, we bring our prayers to you with
confidence, in the name of our Lord Jesus.
In your mercy, Lord, hear our prayer.

Your presence and your reign are already with
us. We pray for ourselves and those dear to us.
(open prayers)

Your kingdom come,
your will be done on earth as in heaven.

Your faithfulness lasts forever. We pray for
our community and for our neighbors.
(open prayers)
Your kingdom come,
your will be done on earth as in heaven.

Your people serve you with gladness. We pray
for the church in all places, that we may know
the freedom of life in the Spirit.
(open prayers)
Your kingdom come,
your will be done on earth as in heaven.

Your way is justice and peace. We pray for the
world and for all who care for creation.
(open prayers)
Your kingdom come,
your will be done on earth as in heaven.

We offer you other concerns we carry in our
hearts.
(open prayers)
Your kingdom come,
your will be done on earth as in heaven.

God of grace and glory,
you keep our souls,
satisfying us with living bread and holy work.
Renew us through forgiveness

and restore us in rest,
that we may look for the coming of your reign
on earth as in heaven.
Secure in your love,
we pray with humility and joy:

Our Father ...

Benediction
*May the God of hope
fill us with all joy and peace in believing
so that we may abound in hope
by the power of the Holy Spirit. Amen.*

Give us today our daily bread

Opening sentence

Give us today our daily bread.
Give us today our daily bread.

Call to praise

Lord, open our lips
and our mouths will proclaim your praise.
You are good to those who wait for you,
to all who seek you.

Glory ...

Psalm 78.18-26

In their heart [the people] put God to the test
by demanding the food they craved.
They even spoke against God.
They said: "Is it possible for God
to prepare a table in the desert?

It was God who struck the rock,
water flowed and swept down in torrents.
But can God also give us bread;
and provide meat for his people?"

On hearing this, the LORD was angry.
A fire was kindled against Jacob,

and anger rose against Israel
for having no faith in God;
for refusing to trust divine help.

Yet God commanded the clouds above
and opened the gates of heaven;
rained down manna for their food,
and gave them bread from heaven.

Mere mortals ate the bread of angels.
The Lord sent them meat in abundance;
made the east wind blow from heaven
and roused the south wind with might.

Thanksgiving

My heart is ready, O God;
I will sing your praise.
Your steadfast love is higher than the heavens,
and your faithfulness reaches to the clouds.
(free prayers of thanksgiving)
Be exalted, O God, above the heavens,
and let your glory shine over all the earth.
Amen.

Song

Asithi: Amen (Sing amen) (H64)
We would extol thee (H74)
Oh, for a thousand tongues to sing (H81)

Call to discipleship

Jesus said, Let anyone with ears to hear listen.
You shall love the Lord your God
with all your heart, and with all your soul,
and with all your strength,
and with all your mind;
and your neighbor as yourself.
Do this, and you will live.
Lord Jesus, you have the words of eternal life.

John 6.(1-7), 8-14

One of [Jesus'] disciples, Andrew, Simon Peter's brother, said to him, "There is a boy here who has five barley loaves and two fish. But what are they among so many people?" Jesus said, "Make the people sit down." Now there was a great deal of grass in the place; so they sat down, about five thousand in all. Then Jesus took the loaves, and when he had given thanks, he distributed them to those who were seated; so also the fish, as much as they wanted. When they were satisfied, he told his disciples, "Gather up the fragments left over, so that nothing may be lost." So they gathered them up, and from the fragments of the five barley loaves, left by those who had eaten, they filled twelve baskets. When the people saw the sign that he had done, they began to say, "This is indeed the prophet who is to come into the world."

Exodus 16.11-15

The LORD spoke to Moses and said, "I have heard the complaining of the Israelites; say to them, 'At twilight you shall eat meat, and in the morning you shall have your fill of bread; then you shall know that I am the LORD your God.'"

In the evening quails came up and covered the camp; and in the morning there was a layer of dew around the camp. When the layer of dew lifted, there on the surface of the wilderness was a fine flaky substance, as fine as frost on the ground. When the Israelites saw it, they said to one another, "What is it?" For they did not know what it was. Moses said to them, "It is the bread that the LORD has given you to eat."

Silent or spoken reflection on the readings

Song
Obey my voice (H163)
God created heaven and earth (H160)
Taste and see (SJ86)

Zechariah's song

*C*all to intercession

Rejoice in the Lord always.
The Lord is near.
Do not worry about anything,
but in everything with thanksgiving
let your requests be made known to God.

God of open hands, we bring our prayers to
you as acts of love for you and for our neighbors.
In your mercy, Lord, hear our prayer.

You provide for all our needs from your bounty. We pray for ourselves and those dear to us.
(open prayers)
Lord, give us today our daily bread.
Give us today our daily bread.

You work wonders in surprising places.
We pray for our community and for our
neighbors.
(open prayers)
Lord, give us today our daily bread.
Give us today our daily bread.

You furnish abundance even from very little.
We pray for the church in all places, that we
may reflect your faithful love.
(open prayers)
Lord, give us today our daily bread.
Give us today our daily bread.

You send forth your Spirit, a breath of renewal
and hope. We pray for the world, for those
who are in need.
(open prayers)
Lord, give us today our daily bread.
Give us today our daily bread.

We offer you other concerns we carry in our
hearts.
(open prayers)
Lord, give us today our daily bread.
Give us today our daily bread.

God of grace and glory,
you fling the stars into the heavens;
you see every sparrow fall.
Deepen our trust in the mystery
of your power shining through Christ Jesus,
that we may live your love for the world.
In the name of the one
who taught us we pray:

Our Father ...

Benediction
*The Lord will guide us continually,
and satisfy our needs in parched places,
and we will be like a watered garden,
like a spring of water,
whose waters never fail. Amen.*

Give us today our daily bread

Opening sentence

Give us today our daily bread.
Give us today our daily bread.

*C*all to praise

O God, your word is a lamp to my feet
and a light to my path.
The light and peace of Jesus Christ be with us.

Glory ...

Psalm 104.27-30

All of these look to you
to give them their food in due season.
You give it, they gather it up;
you open your hand, they have their fill.

You hide your face, they are dismayed;
you take back your spirit, they die,
returning to the dust from which they came.
You send forth your spirit, they are created;
and you renew the face of the earth.

Thanksgiving

It is good to give thanks to the Lord,
to sing praises to your name, O Most High.

(free prayers of thanksgiving)
We declare your steadfast love in the morning,
and your faithfulness by night. Amen.

Song

Let all creation bless the Lord (H61)
Cantemos al Señor (Let's sing unto the
   Lord) (H55)
Spirit, working in creation (SJ10)

Confession

Have mercy on me, O God,
according to your steadfast love;
according to your abundant mercy
blot out my transgressions.
(silence)
Create in me a clean heart, O God,
and put a new and right spirit within me.
Restore to me the joy of your salvation
and sustain in me a willing spirit. Amen.

Call to discipleship

Jesus said, I am the bread of life.
Whoever comes to me will never be hungry,
and whoever believes in me
will never be thirsty.
Lord Jesus, you have the words of eternal life.

Luke 12.22-31

[Jesus] said to his disciples, "Therefore I tell you, do not worry about your life, what you will eat, or about your body, what you will wear. For life is more than food, and the body more than clothing. Consider the ravens: they neither sow nor reap, they have neither store-house nor barn, and yet God feeds them. Of how much more value are you than the birds! And can any of you by worrying add a single hour to your span of life? If then you are not able to do so small a thing as that, why do you worry about the rest? Consider the lilies, how they grow: they neither toil nor spin; yet I tell you, even Solomon in all his glory was not clothed like one of these. But if God so clothes the grass of the field, which is alive today and tomorrow is thrown into the oven, how much more will he clothe you—you of little faith! And do not keep striving for what you are to eat and what you are to drink, and do not keep worrying. For it is the nations of the world that strive after all these things, and your Father knows that you need them. Instead, strive for his kingdom, and these things will be given to you as well."

1 Kings 17.8-16

Then the word of the LORD came to [Elijah], saying, "Go now to Zarephath, which belongs

to Sidon, and live there; for I have commanded a widow there to feed you." So he set out
and went to Zarephath. When he came to the
gate of the town, a widow was there gathering
sticks; he called to her and said, "Bring me a
little water in a vessel, so that I may drink."
As she was going to bring it, he called to her
and said, "Bring me a morsel of bread in your
hand." But she said, "As the LORD your God
lives, I have nothing baked, only a handful of
meal in a jar, and a little oil in a jug; I am now
gathering a couple of sticks, so that I may go
home and prepare it for myself and my son,
that we may eat it, and die." Elijah said to her,
"Do not be afraid; go and do as you have said;
but first make me a little cake of it and bring
it to me, and afterwards make something for
yourself and your son. For thus says the LORD
the God of Israel: The jar of meal will not be
emptied and the jug of oil will not fail until
the day that the LORD sends rain on the earth."
She went and did as Elijah said, so that she
as well as he and her household ate for many
days. The jar of meal was not emptied, neither
did the jug of oil fail, according to the word of
the LORD that he spoke by Elijah.

Silent or spoken reflection on the readings

Song

Why should I feel discouraged (SJ103)
You are all we have (SJ29)
All will be well (SJ98)

Mary's *or* Simeon's song

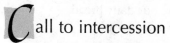

*C*all to intercession

Ask, and it will be given you;
search, and you will find;
knock, and the door will be opened for you.
*The heavenly Father will give the Holy Spirit
to those who ask.*

God of open hands, we bring our prayers to
you with confidence, in the name of our Lord
Jesus.
In your mercy, Lord, hear our prayer.

You provide for all our needs from your bounty. We pray for ourselves and those dear to us.
(open prayers)
Lord, give us today our daily bread.
Give us today our daily bread.

You work wonders in surprising places.
We pray for our community and for our
neighbors.
(open prayers)

Lord, give us today our daily bread.
Give us today our daily bread.

You furnish abundance even from very little.
We pray for the church in all places, that we
may reflect your faithful love.
(open prayers)
Lord, give us today our daily bread.
Give us today our daily bread.

You send forth your Spirit, a breath of renewal
and hope. We pray for the world, for those
who are in need.
(open prayers)
Lord, give us today our daily bread.
Give us today our daily bread.

We offer you other concerns we carry in our
hearts.
(open prayers)
Lord, give us today our daily bread.
Give us today our daily bread.

God of grace and glory, you keep our souls,
satisfying us with living bread and holy work.
Renew us through forgiveness
and restore us in rest,
that we may look for the coming of your reign
on earth as in heaven.
Secure in your love,
we pray with humility and joy:

Our Father ...

Benediction
*The Lord will guide us continually,
and satisfy our needs in parched places,
and we will be like a watered garden,
like a spring of water,
whose waters never fail. Amen.*

Forgive us our sins

Opening sentence

Forgive us our sins
as we forgive those who sin against us.

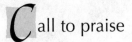

Call to praise

Lord, open our lips
and our mouths will proclaim your praise.
You are good to those who wait for you,
to all who seek you.

Glory ...

Psalm 103.8-14

The LORD is compassion and love,
slow to anger and rich in mercy.
The LORD will not always chide,
will not be angry forever.
God does not treat us according to our sins
nor repay us according to our faults.

For as the heavens are high above the earth
so strong is God's love for the God-fearing;
As far as the east is from the west
so far does he remove our sins.

As parents have compassion on their children,
the LORD has pity on those
    who are God-fearing
for he knows of what we are made,
and remembers that we are dust.

Thanksgiving

My heart is ready, O God;
I will sing your praise.
Your steadfast love is higher than the heavens,
and your faithfulness reaches to the clouds.
(free prayers of thanksgiving)
Be exalted, O God, above the heavens,
and let your glory shine over all the earth.
Amen.

Song

Sing praise to God who reigns (H59)
Great is the Lord (H87)
Great is thy faithfulness (H327)

Call to discipleship

Jesus said, Let anyone with ears to hear listen.
You shall love the Lord your God
with all your heart, and with all your soul,
and with all your strength,
and with all your mind;
and your neighbor as yourself.

Do this, and you will live.
Lord Jesus, you have the words of eternal life.

Mark 11.25

"Whenever you stand praying, forgive, if you have anything against anyone; so that your Father in heaven may also forgive you your trespasses."

Ephesians 4:30–5:2

And do not grieve the Holy Spirit of God, with which you were marked with a seal for the day of redemption. Put away from you all bitterness and wrath and anger and wrangling and slander, together with all malice, and be kind to one another, tenderhearted, forgiving one another, as God in Christ has forgiven you. Therefore be imitators of God, as beloved children, and live in love, as Christ loved us and gave himself up for us, a fragrant offering and sacrifice to God.

Silent or spoken reflection on the readings

Song

Like a mother who has borne us (SJ91)
Beloved, God's chosen (SJ38)
Forgive our sins as we forgive (H137)

Zechariah's song

*C*all to intercession

Rejoice in the Lord always.
The Lord is near.
Do not worry about anything,
but in everything with thanksgiving
let your requests be made known to God.

Merciful God, we bring our prayers to you as
acts of love for you and for our neighbors.
In your mercy, Lord, hear our prayer.

You wipe away our offenses. We pray for ourselves and those dear to us.
(open prayers)
Forgive us our sins
as we forgive those who sin against us.

You speak your word of forgiveness. We pray
for our community and for our neighbors.
(open prayers)
Forgive us our sins
as we forgive those who sin against us.

You have forgiven your people, and you call
us to forgive. We pray for the church in all
places, that we may bear witness to your reign
of justice, peace, and joy.
(open prayers)
Forgive us our sins
as we forgive those who sin against us.

You have reconciled the world to yourself in
Christ. We pray for the world, for all who are
ensnared in greed, violence, and oppression.
(open prayers)
Forgive us our sins
as we forgive those who sin against us.

We offer you other concerns we carry in our
hearts.
(open prayers)
Forgive us our sins
as we forgive those who sin against us.

God of grace and glory,
you fling the stars into the heavens;
you see every sparrow fall.
Deepen our trust in the mystery
of your power shining through Christ Jesus,
that we may live your love for the world.
In the name of the one
who taught us we pray:

Our Father …

Benediction
*Now may the Lord of peace give us peace
at all times in all ways.
The Lord be with us. Amen.*

As we forgive

Opening sentence
Forgive us our sins
as we forgive those who sin against us.

Call to praise

O God, your word is a lamp to my feet
and a light to my path.
The light and peace of Jesus Christ be with us.

Glory ...

Psalm 65.2-5 [1-4]
To you our praise is due
in Zion, O God.
*To you we pay our vows,
you who hear our prayer.*

To you all flesh will come
with its burden of sin.
*Too heavy for us, our offenses,
but you wipe them away.*

Blessed those whom you choose and call
to dwell in your courts.
*We are filled with the blessings of your house,
of your holy temple.*

Thanksgiving

It is good to give thanks to the Lord,
to sing praises to your name, O Most High.
(free prayers of thanksgiving)
We declare your steadfast love in the morning,
and your faithfulness by night. Amen.

Song

Praise, my soul, the God of heaven (H63)
O worship the Lord (H124)
O Lord, our Lord, how majestic (H112)

Confession

Have mercy on me, O God,
according to your steadfast love;
according to your abundant mercy
blot out my transgressions.
(silence)
Create in me a clean heart, O God,
and put a new and right spirit within me.
Restore to me the joy of your salvation
and sustain in me a willing spirit. Amen.

*C*all to discipleship

Jesus said, I am the bread of life.
Whoever comes to me will never be hungry,
and whoever believes in me
will never be thirsty.
Lord Jesus, you have the words of eternal life.

Luke 7.(36-39), 40-50

Jesus spoke up and said to him, "Simon, I have something to say to you." "Teacher," he replied, "Speak." "A certain creditor had two debtors; one owed five hundred denarii, and the other fifty. When they could not pay, he canceled the debts for both of them. Now which of them will love him more?" Simon answered, "I suppose the one for whom he canceled the greater debt." And Jesus said to him, "You have judged rightly." Then turning toward the woman, he said to Simon, "Do you see this woman? I entered your house; you gave me no water for my feet, but she has bathed my feet with her tears and dried them with her hair. You gave me no kiss, but from the time I came in she has not stopped kissing my feet. You did not anoint my head with oil, but she has anointed my feet with ointment. Therefore, I tell you, her sins, which were many, have been forgiven; hence she has shown great love. But the one to whom little is forgiven, loves little." Then he said to her, "Your sins are forgiven." But those who were at the table with him began to say among themselves, "Who is this who even forgives sins?" And he said to the woman, "Your faith has saved you; go in peace."

2 Corinthians 2.5-11

But if anyone has caused pain, he has caused it not to me [Paul], but to some extent—not to exaggerate it—to all of you. This punishment by the majority is enough for such a person; so now instead you should forgive and console him, so that he may not be overwhelmed by excessive sorrow. So I urge you to reaffirm your love for him. I wrote for this reason: to test you and to know whether you are obedient in everything. Anyone whom you forgive, I also forgive. What I have forgiven, if I have forgiven anything, has been for your sake in the presence of Christ. And we do this so that we may not be outwitted by Satan; for we are not ignorant of his designs.

Silent or spoken reflection on the readings

Song

Marvelous grace of our loving Lord (H151)
Great God of wonders (H149)
Lamb of God (SJ21)

Mary's *or* Simeon's song

*C*all to intercession

Ask, and it will be given you;
search, and you will find;
knock, and the door will be opened for you.
The heavenly Father will give the Holy Spirit
to those who ask.

Merciful God, we bring our prayers to you
with confidence, in the name of our Lord
Jesus.
In your mercy, Lord, hear our prayer.

You wipe away our offenses. We pray for ourselves and those dear to us.
(open prayers)
Forgive us our sins
as we forgive those who sin against us.

You speak your word of forgiveness. We pray
for our community and for our neighbors.
(open prayers)
Forgive us our sins
as we forgive those who sin against us.

You have forgiven your people, and you call
us to forgive. We pray for the church in all
places, that we may bear witness to your reign
of justice, peace, and joy.
(open prayers)

Forgive us our sins
as we forgive those who sin against us.

You have reconciled the world to yourself in
Christ. We pray for the world, for all who are
ensnared in greed, violence, and oppression.
(open prayers)
Forgive us our sins
as we forgive those who sin against us.

We offer you other concerns we carry in our
hearts.
(open prayers)
Forgive us our sins
as we forgive those who sin against us.

God of grace and glory, you keep our souls,
satisfying us with living bread and holy work.
Renew us through forgiveness
and restore us in rest,
that we may look for the coming of your reign
on earth as in heaven.
Secure in your love,
we pray with humility and joy:

Our Father …

Benediction
*Now may the Lord of peace give us peace
at all times in all ways.
The Lord be with us. Amen.*

Save us from the time of trial

WEEK 1 LORD'S PRAYER

Opening sentence

Save us from the time of trial.
Save us from the time of trial.

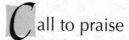all to praise

Lord, open our lips
and our mouths will proclaim your praise.
You are good to those who wait for you,
to all who seek you.

Glory ...

Psalm 25.16-21

Turn to me and have mercy
for I am lonely and poor.

Relieve the anguish of my heart
and set me free from my distress.
See my affliction and my toil
and take all my sins away.

See how many are my foes,
how violent their hatred for me.
Preserve my life and rescue me.
Do not disappoint me, you are my refuge.

May innocence and uprightness protect me,
for my hope is in you, O LORD.

Thanksgiving

My heart is ready, O God;
I will sing your praise.
Your steadfast love is higher than the heavens,
and your faithfulness reaches to the clouds.
(free prayers of thanksgiving)
Be exalted, O God, above the heavens,
and let your glory shine over all the earth.
Amen.

Song

Je louerai l'Eternel (Praise, I will praise you,
   Lord) (H76)
O God, our help in ages past (H328)
God is our refuge and strength (SJ26)

*C*all to discipleship

Jesus said, Let anyone with ears to hear listen.
You shall love the Lord your God
with all your heart, and with all your soul,
and with all your strength,
and with all your mind;
and your neighbor as yourself.
Do this, and you will live.
Lord Jesus, you have the words of eternal life.

Matthew 26.36-39

Then Jesus went with them to a place called Gethsemane; and he said to his disciples, "Sit here while I go over there and pray." He took with him Peter and the two sons of Zebedee, and began to be grieved and agitated. Then he said to them, "I am deeply grieved, even to death; remain here, and stay awake with me." And going a little farther, he threw himself on the ground and prayed, "My Father, if it is possible, let this cup pass from me; yet not what I want but what you want."

1 Corinthians 10.12-13

So if you think you are standing, watch out that you do not fall. No testing has overtaken you that is not common to everyone. God is faithful, and he will not let you be tested beyond your strength, but with the testing he will also provide the way out so that you may be able to endure it.

Silent or spoken reflection on the readings

Song

By gracious powers (H552)
Lord, thou hast searched me (H556)
Don't be afraid (SJ105)

Zechariah's song

*C*all to intercession

Rejoice in the Lord always.
The Lord is near.
Do not worry about anything,
but in everything with thanksgiving
let your requests be made known to God.

Savior God, we bring our prayers to you as
acts of love for you and for our neighbors.
In your mercy, Lord, hear our prayer.

Your power protects us in times of trouble. We
pray for ourselves and those dear to us.
(open prayers)
Save us from the time of trial, Lord.
Save us from the time of trial.

Your Spirit comforts those who endure trials.
We pray for our community and for our
neighbors.
(open prayers)
Save us from the time of trial, Lord.
Save us from the time of trial.

You hold your people securely in your care.
We pray for the church in all places, that we
may daily follow in the footsteps of Christ.
(open prayers)
Save us from the time of trial, Lord.
Save us from the time of trial.

You alone are worthy of trust. We pray for
the world, for those in positions of power and
authority.
(open prayers)
Save us from the time of trial, Lord.
Save us from the time of trial.

We offer you other concerns we carry in our
hearts.
(open prayers)
Save us from the time of trial, Lord.
Save us from the time of trial.

God of grace and glory,
you fling the stars into the heavens;
you see every sparrow fall.
Deepen our trust in the mystery
of your power shining through Christ Jesus,
that we may live your love for the world.
In the name of the one
who taught us we pray:

Our Father ...

Benediction
The Lord will keep us from all evil.
The Lord will keep our life.
The Lord will keep our going out
and our coming in
from this time on and forevermore. Amen.

Save us from the time of trial

Opening sentence
Save us from the time of trial.
Save us from the time of trial.

*C*all to praise

O God, your word is a lamp to my feet
and a light to my path.
The light and peace of Jesus Christ be with us.

Glory ...

Psalm 31.10-16 [9-15]
Have mercy on me, O LORD,
for I am in distress.
Tears have wasted my eyes,
my throat and my heart.

For my life is spent with sorrow
and my years with sighs.
Affliction has broken down my strength
and my bones waste away.

In the face of all my foes
I am a reproach,
an object of scorn to my neighbors
and of fear to my friends.

Those who see me in the street
run far away from me.
I am like the dead, forgotten by all,
like a thing thrown away.

I have heard the slander of the crowd,
fear is all around me,
as they plot together against me,
as they plan to take my life.

But as for me, I trust in you, LORD;
I say: "You are my God.
My life is in your hands, deliver me
from the hands of those who hate me."

Thanksgiving

It is good to give thanks to the Lord,
to sing praises to your name, O Most High.
(free prayers of thanksgiving)
We declare your steadfast love in the morning,
and your faithfulness by night. Amen.

Song

In thee is gladness (H114)
Oh, for a thousand tongues to sing (H110)
Now thank we all our God (H86)

Confession

Have mercy on me, O God,
according to your steadfast love;

according to your abundant mercy
blot out my transgressions.
(silence)
Create in me a clean heart, O God,
and put a new and right spirit within me.
Restore to me the joy of your salvation
and sustain in me a willing spirit. Amen.

Call to discipleship

Jesus said, I am the bread of life.
Whoever comes to me will never be hungry,
and whoever believes in me
will never be thirsty.
Lord Jesus, you have the words of eternal life.

Matthew 26.40-46

Then [Jesus] came to the disciples and found
them sleeping; and he said to Peter, "So, could
you not stay awake with me one hour? Stay
awake and pray that you may not come into
the time of trial; the spirit indeed is willing,
but the flesh is weak." Again he went away
for the second time and prayed, "My Father, if
this cannot pass unless I drink it, your will be
done." Again he came and found them sleeping, for their eyes were heavy. So leaving them
again, he went away and prayed for the third
time, saying the same words. Then he came to

the disciples and said to them, "Are you still sleeping and taking your rest? See, the hour is at hand, and the Son of Man is betrayed into the hands of sinners. Get up, let us be going. See, my betrayer is at hand."

James 1.12-15

Blessed is anyone who endures temptation. Such a one has stood the test and will receive the crown of life that the Lord has promised to those who love him. No one, when tempted, should say, "I am being tempted by God"; for God cannot be tempted by evil and he himself tempts no one. But one is tempted by one's own desire, being lured and enticed by it; then, when that desire has conceived, it gives birth to sin, and that sin, when it is fully grown, gives birth to death.

Silent or spoken reflection on the readings

Song

All will be well (SJ98)
O Holy Spirit, Root of life (H123)
When from the darkness (SJ102)

Mary's *or* Simeon's song

*C*all to intercession

Ask, and it will be given you;
search, and you will find;
knock, and the door will be opened for you.
The heavenly Father will give the Holy Spirit
to those who ask.

Savior God, we bring our prayers to you with
confidence, in the name of our Lord Jesus.
In your mercy, Lord, hear our prayer.

Your power protects us in times of trouble. We
pray for ourselves and those dear to us.
(open prayers)
Save us from the time of trial, Lord.
Save us from the time of trial.

Your Spirit comforts those who endure trials.
We pray for our community and for our
neighbors.
(open prayers)
Save us from the time of trial, Lord.
Save us from the time of trial.

You hold your people securely in your care.
We pray for the church in all places, that we
may daily follow in the footsteps of Christ.
(open prayers)
Save us from the time of trial, Lord.
Save us from the time of trial.

You alone are worthy of trust. We pray for
the world, for those in positions of power and
authority.
(open prayers)
Save us from the time of trial, Lord.
Save us from the time of trial.

We offer you other concerns we carry in our
hearts.
(open prayers)
Save us from the time of trial, Lord.
Save us from the time of trial.

God of grace and glory, you keep our souls,
satisfying us with living bread and holy work.
Renew us through forgiveness
and restore us in rest,
that we may look for the coming of your reign
on earth as in heaven.
Secure in your love,
we pray with humility and joy:

Our Father ...

Benediction
The Lord will keep us from all evil.
The Lord will keep our life.
The Lord will keep our going out
and our coming in
from this time on and forevermore. Amen.

Deliver us from evil

Opening sentence

Deliver us from evil.
Deliver us from evil.

Call to praise

Lord, open our lips
and our mouths will proclaim your praise.
You are good to those who wait for you,
to all who seek you.

Glory ...

Psalm 140.2-8 [1-7]

Rescue me, LORD, from the wicked;
from the violent keep me safe,
from those who plan evil in their hearts
and stir up strife every day;
who sharpen their tongue like an adder's,
with the poison of viper on their lips.

LORD, guard me from the hands of the wicked;
from the violent keep me safe;
they plan to make me stumble.
The proud have hidden a trap,

have spread out lines in a net,
set snares across my path.

I have said to the LORD: "You are my God."
LORD, hear the cry of my appeal!
LORD my God, my mighty help,
you shield my head in the battle.

Thanksgiving

My heart is ready, O God;
I will sing your praise.
Your steadfast love is higher than the heavens,
and your faithfulness reaches to the clouds.
(free prayers of thanksgiving)
Be exalted, O God, above the heavens,
and let your glory shine over all the earth.
Amen.

Song

Confitemini Domino (Come and fill our
hearts) (SJ59)
O worship the King (H66)
You are all we have (SJ29)

*C*all to discipleship

Jesus said, Let anyone with ears to hear listen.
You shall love the Lord your God
with all your heart, and with all your soul,
and with all your strength,

and with all your mind;
and your neighbor as yourself.
Do this, and you will live.
Lord Jesus, you have the words of eternal life.

Matthew 4.1-7

Then Jesus was led up by the Spirit into the wilderness to be tempted by the devil. He fasted forty days and forty nights, and afterwards he was famished. The tempter came and said to him, "If you are the Son of God, command these stones to become loaves of bread." But he answered, "It is written,

> 'One does not live by bread alone,
>> but by every word that comes from the
>> mouth of God.'"

Then the devil took him to the holy city and placed him on the pinnacle of the temple, saying to him, "If you are the Son of God, throw yourself down; for it is written,

> 'He will command his angels concerning
>> you,'
> and 'On their hands they will bear you up,
> so that you will not dash your foot against
>> a stone.'"

Jesus said to him, "Again it is written, 'Do not put the Lord your God to the test.'"

Hebrews 2.14-18

Since, therefore, the children share flesh and blood, [Christ] himself likewise shared the same things, so that through death he might destroy the one who has the power of death, that is, the devil, and free those who all their lives were held in slavery by the fear of death. For it is clear that he did not come to help angels, but the descendants of Abraham. Therefore he had to become like his brothers and sisters in every respect, so that he might be a merciful and faithful high priest in the service of God, to make a sacrifice of atonement for the sins of the people. Because he himself was tested by what he suffered, he is able to help those who are being tested.

Silent or spoken reflection on the readings

Song

And I will raise you up (H596, with verses)
Here I am (SJ100)
Fount of love, our Savior God (H354)

Zechariah's song

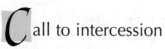 **all to intercession**

Rejoice in the Lord always.
The Lord is near.

Do not worry about anything,
but in everything with thanksgiving
let your requests be made known to God.

God, our help, we bring our prayers to you as
acts of love for you and for our neighbors.
In your mercy, Lord, hear our prayer.

You guard us in our need. We pray for ourselves and those dear to us.
(open prayers)
Deliver us from evil, Lord.
Deliver us from evil.

You are able to help those who are being tested. We pray for our community and for our
neighbors.
(open prayers)
Deliver us from evil, Lord.
Deliver us from evil.

You enable your people to stand firm. We
pray for the church in all places, that we may
speak boldly for Christ.
(open prayers)
Deliver us from evil, Lord.
Deliver us from evil.

You loosen the grip of the unjust, of the
oppressor. We pray for the world, for all who
do justice and love mercy.
(open prayers)

Deliver us from evil, Lord.
Deliver us from evil.

We offer you other concerns we carry in our
hearts.
(open prayers)
Deliver us from evil, Lord.
Deliver us from evil.

God of grace and glory,
you fling the stars into the heavens;
you see every sparrow fall.
Deepen our trust in the mystery
of your power shining through Christ Jesus,
that we may live your love for the world.
In the name of the one
who taught us we pray:

Our Father ...

Benediction

The peace of God,
which surpasses all understanding,
will guard our hearts and our minds
in Christ Jesus. Amen.

Deliver us from evil

Opening sentence

Deliver us from evil.
Deliver us from evil.

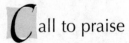all to praise

O God, your word is a lamp to my feet
and a light to my path.
The light and peace of Jesus Christ be with us.

Glory ...

Psalm 71.1-4

In you, O LORD, I take refuge;
let me never be put to shame.
In your justice rescue me, free me;
pay heed to me and save me.

Be a rock where I can take refuge,
a mighty stronghold to save me;
for you are my rock, my stronghold.
Free me from the hand of the wicked,
from the grip of the unjust, of the oppressor.

Thanksgiving

It is good to give thanks to the Lord,
to sing praises to your name, O Most High.

(free prayers of thanksgiving)
We declare your steadfast love in the morning,
and your faithfulness by night. Amen.

Song

All glory be to God on high (H122)
We worship God the Rock (SJ28)
What mercy and divine compassion (H524)

Confession

Have mercy on me, O God,
according to your steadfast love;
according to your abundant mercy
blot out my transgressions.
(silence)
Create in me a clean heart, O God,
and put a new and right spirit within me.
Restore to me the joy of your salvation
and sustain in me a willing spirit. Amen.

*C*all to discipleship

Jesus said, I am the bread of life.
Whoever comes to me will never be hungry,
and whoever believes in me
will never be thirsty.
Lord Jesus, you have the words of eternal life.

Matthew 4.8-11

Again, the devil took [Jesus] to a very high mountain and showed him all the kingdoms of the world and their splendor; and he said to him, "All these I will give you, if you will fall down and worship me." Jesus said to him, "Away with you, Satan! for it is written,

'Worship the Lord your God,
and serve only him.'"

Then the devil left him, and suddenly angels came and waited on him.

Ephesians 6.10-13, (14-18)

Finally, be strong in the Lord and in the strength of his power. Put on the whole armor of God, so that you may be able to stand against the wiles of the devil. For our struggle is not against enemies of blood and flesh, but against the rulers, against the authorities, against the cosmic powers of this present darkness, against the spiritual forces of evil in the heavenly places. Therefore take up the whole armor of God, so that you may be able to withstand on that evil day, and having done everything, to stand firm.

Silent or spoken reflection on the readings

Song

In the stillness of the evening (H551)

If you but trust in God (H576)
All will be well (SJ98)

Mary's *or* Simeon's song

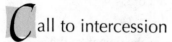# *C*all to intercession

Ask, and it will be given you;
search, and you will find;
knock, and the door will be opened for you.
The heavenly Father will give the Holy Spirit
to those who ask.

God, our help, we bring our prayers to you
with confidence, in the name of our Lord
Jesus.
In your mercy, Lord, hear our prayer.

You guard us in our need. We pray for ourselves and those dear to us.
(open prayers)
Deliver us from evil, Lord.
Deliver us from evil.

You are able to help those who are being tested. We pray for our community and for our
neighbors.
(open prayers)
Deliver us from evil, Lord.
Deliver us from evil.

You enable your people to stand firm. We
pray for the church in all places, that we may
speak boldly for Christ.
(open prayers)
Deliver us from evil, Lord.
Deliver us from evil.

You loosen the grip of the unjust, of the
oppressor. We pray for the world, for all who
do justice and love mercy.
(open prayers)
Deliver us from evil, Lord.
Deliver us from evil.

We offer you other concerns we carry in our
hearts.
(open prayers)
Deliver us from evil, Lord.
Deliver us from evil.

God of grace and glory,
you keep our souls,
satisfying us with living bread and holy work.
Renew us through forgiveness
and restore us in rest,
that we may look for the coming of your reign
on earth as in heaven.
Secure in your love,
we pray with humility and joy:

Our Father ...

Benediction

The peace of God,
which surpasses all understanding,
will guard our hearts and our minds
in Christ Jesus. Amen.

The kingdom, the power, and the glory are yours

Opening sentence

For the kingdom, the power,
and the glory are yours
now and forever.

Call to praise

Lord, open our lips
and our mouths will proclaim your praise.
You are good to those who wait for you,
to all who seek you.

Glory …

Psalm 145.10-14

All your creatures shall thank you, O LORD,
and your friends shall repeat their blessing.
They shall speak of the glory of your reign
and declare your might, O God,

to make known to all your mighty deeds
and the glorious splendor of your reign.
Yours is an everlasting kingdom;
your rule lasts from age to age.

You are faithful in all your words
and loving in all your deeds.
You support all those who are falling
and raise up all who are bowed down.

Thanksgiving

My heart is ready, O God;
I will sing your praise.
Your steadfast love is higher than the heavens,
and your faithfulness reaches to the clouds.
(free prayers of thanksgiving)
Be exalted, O God, above the heavens,
and let your glory shine over all the earth.
Amen.

Song

Praise to the Lord, the Almighty (H37)
Joyful, joyful, we adore thee (H71)
Let the whole creation cry (H51)

Call to discipleship

Jesus said, Let anyone with ears to hear listen.
You shall love the Lord your God
with all your heart, and with all your soul,
and with all your strength,
and with all your mind;
and your neighbor as yourself.
Do this, and you will live.
Lord Jesus, you have the words of eternal life.

Mark 1.14-15

Now after John was arrested, Jesus came to Galilee, proclaiming the good news of God, and saying, "The time is fulfilled, and the kingdom of God has come near; repent, and believe in the good news."

Revelation 4.9-11

And whenever the living creatures give glory and honor and thanks to the one who is seated on the throne, who lives forever and ever, the twenty-four elders fall before the one who is seated on the throne and worship the one who lives forever and ever; they cast their crowns before the throne, singing,

"You are worthy, our Lord and God,
to receive glory and honor and power,
for you created all things,
and by your will they existed and were
created."

Silent or spoken reflection on the readings

Song

Crown him with many crowns (H116)
Blessing and honor and glory (H108)
Here from all nations (H296)

Zechariah's song

Call to intercession

Rejoice in the Lord always.
The Lord is near.
Do not worry about anything,
but in everything with thanksgiving
let your requests be made known to God.

God of immeasurable greatness, we bring our
prayers to you as acts of love for you and for
our neighbors.
In your mercy, Lord, hear our prayer.

You create in us clean hearts and willing spirits. We pray for ourselves and those dear to
us.
(open prayers)
For the kingdom, the power,
and the glory are yours
now and forever.

You support those who are falling. We pray
for our community and for our neighbors.
(open prayers)
For the kingdom, the power,
and the glory are yours
now and forever.

You surround your people with a great cloud
of witnesses. We pray for the church in all

places, that we may be faithful in solidarity
across generations and geography.
(open prayers)
For the kingdom, the power,
and the glory are yours
now and forever.

You alone are worthy to receive honor and
praise. We pray for the world, for our enemies
and for those who are in conflict.
(open prayers)
For the kingdom, the power,
and the glory are yours
now and forever.

We offer you other concerns we carry in our
hearts.
(open prayers)
For the kingdom, the power,
and the glory are yours
now and forever.

God of grace and glory,
you fling the stars into the heavens;
you see every sparrow fall.
Deepen our trust in the mystery
of your power shining through Christ Jesus,
that we may live your love for the world.
In the name of the one
who taught us we pray:

Our Father ...

Benediction

Peace be to the whole community,
and love with faith,
from God the Father
and the Lord Jesus Christ. Amen.

Now and forever

Opening sentence

For the kingdom, the power,
and the glory are yours
now and forever.

Call to praise

O God, your word is a lamp to my feet
and a light to my path.
The light and peace of Jesus Christ be with us.

Glory ...

Psalm 145.1-9

I will give you glory, O God my king,
I will bless your name for ever.

I will bless you day after day
and praise your name for ever.
You are great, LORD, highly to be praised,
your greatness cannot be measured.

Age to age shall proclaim your works,
shall declare your mighty deeds,
shall speak of your splendor and glory,
tell the tale of your wonderful works.

They will speak of your terrible deeds,
recount your greatness and might.
They will recall your abundant goodness;
age to age shall ring out your justice.

You are kind and full of compassion,
slow to anger, abounding in love.
How good you are, Lord, to all,
compassionate to all your creatures.

Thanksgiving

It is good to give thanks to the Lord,
to sing praises to your name, O Most High.
(free prayers of thanksgiving)
We declare your steadfast love in the morning,
and your faithfulness by night. Amen.

Song

We give thanks unto you (H161)
All creatures of our God and King (H48)
O bless the Lord, my soul (H80)

Confession

Have mercy on me, O God,
according to your steadfast love;
according to your abundant mercy
blot out my transgressions.
(silence)
Create in me a clean heart, O God,
and put a new and right spirit within me.

Restore to me the joy of your salvation
and sustain in me a willing spirit. Amen.

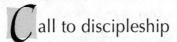all to discipleship

Jesus said, I am the bread of life.
Whoever comes to me will never be hungry,
and whoever believes in me
will never be thirsty.
Lord Jesus, you have the words of eternal life.

Luke 23.42-43

Then [the criminal] said, "Jesus, remember
me when you come into your kingdom." He
replied, "Truly I tell you, today you will be
with me in Paradise."

Hebrews 12.1-2

Therefore, since we are surrounded by so
great a cloud of witnesses, let us also lay aside
every weight and the sin that clings so closely,
and let us run with perseverance the race that
is set before us, looking to Jesus the pioneer
and perfecter of our faith, who for the sake of
the joy that was set before him endured the
cross, disregarding its shame, and has taken
his seat at the right hand of the throne of God.

Silent or spoken reflection on the readings

Song

Christ is the world's true light (H334)
Jesus, remember me (H247)
Sing with all the saints (SS92)

Mary's *or* Simeon's song

*C*all to intercession

Ask, and it will be given you;
search, and you will find;
knock, and the door will be opened for you.
***The heavenly Father will give the Holy Spirit
to those who ask.***

God of immeasurable greatness, we bring our
prayers to you with confidence, in the name
of our Lord Jesus.
In your mercy, Lord, hear our prayer.

You create in us clean hearts and willing spirits. We pray for ourselves and those dear to
us.
(open prayers)
For the kingdom, the power,
and the glory are yours
now and forever.

You support those who are falling. We pray
for our community and for our neighbors.
(open prayers)

For the kingdom, the power,
and the glory are yours
now and forever.

You surround your people with a great cloud
of witnesses. We pray for the church in all
places, that we may be faithful in solidarity
across generations and geography.
(open prayers)
For the kingdom, the power,
and the glory are yours
now and forever.

You alone are worthy to receive honor and
praise. We pray for the world, for our enemies
and for those who are in conflict.
(open prayers)
For the kingdom, the power,
and the glory are yours
now and forever.

We offer you other concerns we carry in our
hearts.
(open prayers)
For the kingdom, the power,
and the glory are yours
now and forever.

God of grace and glory,
you keep our souls,
satisfying us with living bread and holy work.
Renew us through forgiveness

and restore us in rest,
that we may look for the coming of your reign
on earth as in heaven.
Secure in your love,
we pray with humility and joy:

Our Father ...

Benediction
Peace be to the whole community,
and love with faith,
from God the Father
and the Lord Jesus Christ. Amen.

WEEK 2

Beatitudes

Blessed are the poor in spirit

WEEK 2 BEATITUDES

Opening sentence

Blessed are the poor in spirit,
for theirs is the kingdom of heaven.

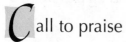all to praise

Lord, open our lips
and our mouths will proclaim your praise.
You are good to those who wait for you,
to all who seek you.

Glory ...

Isaiah 57.14-15

It shall be said,
"Build up, build up, prepare the way,
remove every obstruction from my people's
   way."
For thus says the high and lofty one
who inhabits eternity, whose name is Holy:
I dwell in the high and holy place,
and also with those who are contrite and
   humble in spirit,
to revive the spirit of the humble,
and to revive the heart of the contrite.

Thanksgiving

My heart is ready, O God;
I will sing your praise.
Your steadfast love is higher than the heavens,
and your faithfulness reaches to the clouds.
(free prayers of thanksgiving)
Be exalted, O God, above the heavens,
and let your glory shine over all the earth.
Amen.

Song

Immortal, invisible, God only wise (H70)
Praise God, the Source of life (H95)
Holy, holy, holy (H120)

Call to discipleship

Jesus said, Let anyone with ears to hear listen.
You shall love the Lord your God
with all your heart, and with all your soul,
and with all your strength,
and with all your mind;
and your neighbor as yourself.
Do this, and you will live.
Lord Jesus, you have the words of eternal life.

Mark 15.47–16.8

Mary Magdalene and Mary the mother of
Jesus saw where [Jesus'] body was laid.

When the sabbath was over, Mary Magdalene, and Mary the mother of James, and Salome bought spices, so that they might go and anoint him. And very early on the first day of the week, when the sun had risen, they went to the tomb. They had been saying to one another, "Who will roll away the stone for us from the entrance to the tomb?" When they looked up, they saw that the stone, which was very large, had already been rolled back. As they entered the tomb, they saw a young man, dressed in a white robe, sitting on the right side; and they were alarmed. But he said to them, "Do not be alarmed; you are looking for Jesus of Nazareth, who was crucified. He has been raised; he is not here. Look, there is the place they laid him. But go, tell his disciples and Peter that he is going ahead of you to Galilee; there you will see him, just as he told you." So they went out and fled from the tomb, for terror and amazement had seized them; and they said nothing to anyone, for they were afraid.

James 4.5-10

Or do you suppose that it is for nothing that the scripture says, "God yearns jealously for the spirit that he has made to dwell in us"? But he gives all the more grace; therefore it says,

"God opposes the proud,
     but gives grace to the humble."
Submit yourselves therefore to God. Resist
the devil, and he will flee from you. Draw
near to God, and he will draw near to you.
Cleanse your hands, you sinners, and purify
your hearts, you double-minded. Lament and
mourn and weep. Let your laughter be turned
into mourning and your joy into dejection.
Humble yourselves before the Lord, and he
will exalt you.

Silent or spoken reflection on the readings

Song
   See the splendor of the morning (H268)
   Thine is the glory (H269)
   How bless'd are they (H525)

The Beatitudes

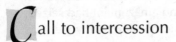

*C*all to intercession

Rejoice in the Lord always.
The Lord is near.
Do not worry about anything,
but in everything with thanksgiving
let your requests be made known to God.

God of the foolish and the despised, we bring our prayers to you as acts of love for you and for our neighbors.
In your mercy, Lord, hear our prayer.

You refresh the spirits of the humble. We pray for ourselves and those dear to us.
(open prayers)
You bless the poor in spirit;
theirs is the kingdom of heaven.

You remind us that those who welcome children welcome you. We pray for our community and for our neighbors.
(open prayers)
You bless the poor in spirit;
theirs is the kingdom of heaven.

You revive the hearts of the contrite. We pray for the church in all places, that we may be one.
(open prayers)
You bless the poor in spirit;
theirs is the kingdom of heaven.

You choose what is foolish in the world to shame the wise. We pray for the world, that your reign may come and your will be done on earth.
(open prayers)
You bless the poor in spirit;
theirs is the kingdom of heaven.

We offer you other concerns we carry in our hearts.
(open prayers)
You bless the poor in spirit;
theirs is the kingdom of heaven.

God whose justice shines like the sun,
you bless all who seek first
your kingdom and righteousness.
Fill our hearts
with the spirit of the Beatitudes,
that we may live this day
in simplicity, mercy, and joy.
Through Jesus,
who taught us to do so,
we pray for the coming of your reign:

Our Father ...

Benediction

Now may the God of peace,
who brought back from the dead
our Lord Jesus,
make us complete in everything good,
so that we may do God's will,
through Jesus Christ,
to whom be the glory forever and ever. Amen.

Blessed are the poor in spirit

WEEK 2 BEATITUDES

Opening sentence

Blessed are the poor in spirit,
for theirs is the kingdom of heaven.

*C*all to praise

O God, your word is a lamp to my feet
and a light to my path.
The light and peace of Jesus Christ be with us.

Glory ...

Psalm 131.1-2

O LORD, my heart is not proud
nor haughty my eyes.
*I have not gone after things too great
nor marvels beyond me.*

Truly I have set my soul
in silence and peace.
*A weaned child on its mother's breast,
even so is my soul.*

Thanksgiving

It is good to give thanks to the Lord,
to sing praises to your name, O Most High.
(free prayers of thanksgiving)

We declare your steadfast love in the morning,
and your faithfulness by night. Amen.

Song

For God so loved us (H167)
Santo (Holy) (SJ15)
Now thank we all our God (H86)

Confession

Have mercy on me, O God,
according to your steadfast love;
according to your abundant mercy
blot out my transgressions.
(*silence*)
Create in me a clean heart, O God,
and put a new and right spirit within me.
Restore to me the joy of your salvation
and sustain in me a willing spirit. Amen.

*C*all to discipleship

Jesus said, I am the bread of life.
Whoever comes to me will never be hungry,
and whoever believes in me
will never be thirsty.
Lord Jesus, you have the words of eternal life.

Matthew 18.1-5

At that time the disciples came to Jesus and
asked, "Who is the greatest in the kingdom

of heaven?" He called a child, whom he put among them, and said, "Truly I tell you, unless you change and become like children, you will never enter the kingdom of heaven. Whoever becomes humble like this child is the greatest in the kingdom of heaven. Whoever welcomes one such child in my name welcomes me."

1 Corinthians 1.26-31

Consider your own call, brothers and sisters: not many of you were wise by human standards, not many were powerful, not many were of noble birth. But God chose what is foolish in the world to shame the wise; God chose what is weak in the world to shame the strong; God chose what is low and despised in the world, things that are not, to reduce to nothing things that are, so that no one might boast in the presence of God. He is the source of your life in Christ Jesus, who became for us wisdom from God, and righteousness and sanctification and redemption, in order that, as it is written, "Let the one who boasts, boast in the Lord."

Silent or spoken reflection on the readings

Song

Oh, blessed are the poor in spirit (H231)

Blest are they (SJ94)
O let all who thirst (H495)

The Beatitudes

Call to intercession

Ask, and it will be given you;
search, and you will find;
knock, and the door will be opened for you.
The heavenly Father will give the Holy Spirit
to those who ask.

God of the foolish and the despised, we bring
our prayers to you with confidence, in the
name of our Lord Jesus.
In your mercy, Lord, hear our prayer.

You refresh the spirits of the humble. We pray
for ourselves and those dear to us.
(open prayers)
You bless the poor in spirit;
theirs is the kingdom of heaven.

You remind us that those who welcome children welcome you. We pray for our community and for our neighbors.
(open prayers)
You bless the poor in spirit;
theirs is the kingdom of heaven.

You revive the hearts of the contrite. We pray
for the church in all places, that we may be
one.
(open prayers)
You bless the poor in spirit;
theirs is the kingdom of heaven.

You choose what is foolish in the world to
shame the wise. We pray for the world, that
your reign may come and your will be done
on earth.
(open prayers)
You bless the poor in spirit;
theirs is the kingdom of heaven.

We offer you other concerns we carry in our
hearts.
(open prayers)
You bless the poor in spirit;
theirs is the kingdom of heaven.

God of compassion and joy,
you satisfy all who hunger
for your righteousness.
Give us grace to endure testing
and be true to your kingdom,
that we may enjoy the life you bless.
Through Jesus,
who taught us to do so,
we pray for the coming of your reign:

Our Father ...

Benediction

Now may the God of peace,
who brought back from the dead
our Lord Jesus,
make us complete in everything good,
so that we may do God's will,
through Jesus Christ,
to whom be the glory forever and ever. Amen.

Blessed are those who mourn

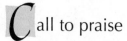

WEEK 2 BEATITUDES

Opening sentence

Blessed are those who mourn,
for they will be comforted.

Call to praise

Lord, open our lips
and our mouths will proclaim your praise.
You are good to those who wait for you,
to all who seek you.

Glory ...

Psalm 126

When the Lord delivered Zion from bondage,
it seemed like a dream.
Then was our mouth filled with laughter,
on our lips there were songs.

The heathens themselves said: "What marvels
the Lord worked for them!"
What marvels the Lord worked for us!
Indeed we were glad.

Deliver us, O Lord, from our bondage
as streams in dry land.

*Those who are sowing in tears
will sing when they reap.*

They go out, they go out, full of tears,
carrying seed for the sowing;
*they come back, they come back, full of song,
carrying their sheaves.*

Thanksgiving

My heart is ready, O God;
I will sing your praise.
*Your steadfast love is higher than the heavens,
and your faithfulness reaches to the clouds.*
(free prayers of thanksgiving)
Be exalted, O God, above the heavens,
*and let your glory shine over all the earth.
Amen.*

Song

From all that dwell below the skies (H49)
In thee is gladness (H114)
Amen (H643)

*C*all to discipleship

Jesus said, Let anyone with ears to hear listen.
*You shall love the Lord your God
with all your heart, and with all your soul,
and with all your strength,*

and with all your mind;
and your neighbor as yourself.
Do this, and you will live.
Lord Jesus, you have the words of eternal life.

John 16.20-22

"Very truly, I tell you, you will weep and mourn, but the world will rejoice; you will have pain, but your pain will turn into joy. When a woman is in labor, she has pain, because her hour has come. But when her child is born, she no longer remembers the anguish because of her joy of having brought a human being into the world. So you have pain now; but I will see you again, and your hearts will rejoice, and no one will take your joy from you."

Revelation 7.13-17

Then one of the elders addressed me [John, your brother], saying, "Who are these, robed in white, and where have they come from?" I said to him, "Sir, you are the one that knows." Then he said to me, "These are they who have come out of the great ordeal; they have washed their robes and made them white in the blood of the Lamb.

For this reason they are before the throne of God,

and worship him day and night within his
    temple,
and the one who is seated on the throne
    will shelter them.
They will hunger no more, and thirst no
    more;
the sun will not strike them,
nor any scorching heat;
for the Lamb at the center of the throne
    will be their shepherd,
and he will guide them to springs of the
    water of life,
and God will wipe away every tear
    from their eyes."

Silent or spoken reflection on the readings

Song
    All glory be to God on high (H122)
    O bless the Lord, my soul (H600)
    Soon and very soon (H611)

The Beatitudes

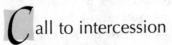

*C*all to intercession

Rejoice in the Lord always.
The Lord is near.

Do not worry about anything,
but in everything with thanksgiving
let your requests be made known to God.

Comforting God, we bring our prayers to you
as acts of love for you and for our neighbors.
In your mercy, Lord, hear our prayer.

Your favor lasts through all our life. We pray
for ourselves and those dear to us.
(open prayers)
You bless those who mourn;
they will be comforted.

You promise that pain will turn to joy.
We pray for our community and for our
neighbors.
(open prayers)
You bless those who mourn;
they will be comforted.

You guide your people to springs of the water
of life. We pray for the church in all places,
that we may know the freedom of life in the
Spirit.
(open prayers)
You bless those who mourn;
they will be comforted.

Your glory will shine over all the earth and
sea. We pray for the world and for all who
care for creation.

(open prayers)
You bless those who mourn;
they will be comforted.

We offer you other concerns we carry in our
hearts.
(open prayers)
You bless those who mourn;
they will be comforted.

God whose justice shines like the sun,
you bless all who seek first
your kingdom and righteousness.
Fill our hearts
with the spirit of the Beatitudes,
that we may live this day
in simplicity, mercy, and joy.
Through Jesus,
who taught us to do so,
we pray for the coming of your reign:

Our Father ...

Benediction

*May the Father of mercies
and the God of all comfort
comfort us in our affliction,
so that we may be able
to comfort those who are afflicted
with the consolation
with which we ourselves are consoled by God.
Amen.*

Blessed are those who mourn

Opening sentence

Blessed are those who mourn,
for they will be comforted.

*C*all to praise

O God, your word is a lamp to my feet
and a light to my path.
The light and peace of Jesus Christ be with us.

Glory ...

Psalm 30.3-6 [2-5]

O LORD, I cried to you for help
and you, my God, have healed me.
O LORD, you have raised my soul
 from the dead,
restored me to life
 from those who sink into the grave.

Sing psalms to the LORD, you faithful ones,
give thanks to his holy name.
God's anger lasts a moment;
 God's favor all through life.
At night there are tears,
 but joy comes with dawn.

Thanksgiving

It is good to give thanks to the Lord,
to sing praises to your name, O Most High.
(free prayers of thanksgiving)
We declare your steadfast love in the morning,
and your faithfulness by night. Amen.

Song

Now, on land and sea descending (H655)
Sing praise to God who reigns (H59)
Praise, my soul, the God of heaven! (H63)

Confession

Have mercy on me, O God,
according to your steadfast love;
according to your abundant mercy
blot out my transgressions.
(silence)
Create in me a clean heart, O God,
and put a new and right spirit within me.
Restore to me the joy of your salvation
and sustain in me a willing spirit. Amen.

Call to discipleship

Jesus said, I am the bread of life.
Whoever comes to me will never be hungry,
and whoever believes in me
will never be thirsty.
Lord Jesus, you have the words of eternal life.

John 11.28-36

[Martha] went back and called her sister
Mary, and told her privately, "The Teacher is
here and is calling for you." And when she
heard it, she got up quickly and went to him.
Now Jesus had not yet come to the village,
but was still at the place where Martha had
met him. The Jews who were with her in the
house, consoling her, saw Mary get up quickly
and go out. They followed her because they
thought that she was going to the tomb to
weep there. When Mary came where Jesus
was and saw him, she knelt at his feet and
said to him, "Lord, if you had been here, my
brother would not have died." When Jesus
saw her weeping, and the Jews who came
with her also weeping, he was greatly disturbed in spirit and deeply moved. He said,
"Where have you laid him?" They said to him,
"Lord, come and see." Jesus began to weep.
So the Jews said, "See how he loved him!"

Isaiah 40.1-2

Comfort, O comfort my people,
says your God.
Speak tenderly to Jerusalem,
and cry to her
that she has served her term,
that her penalty is paid,

that she has received from the LORD's hand
double for all her sins.

Silent or spoken reflection on the readings

Song
Jesus, lover of my soul (H618)
When in the hour of deepest need (H131)
God remembers (SJ107)

The Beatitudes

*C*all to intercession

Ask, and it will be given you;
search, and you will find;
knock, and the door will be opened for you.
*The heavenly Father will give the Holy Spirit
to those who ask.*

Comforting God, we bring our prayers to
you with confidence, in the name of our Lord
Jesus.
In your mercy, Lord, hear our prayer.

Your favor lasts through all our life. We pray
for ourselves and those dear to us.
(open prayers)
You bless those who mourn;
they will be comforted.

You promise that pain will turn to joy.
We pray for our community and for our
neighbors.
(open prayers)
You bless those who mourn;
they will be comforted.

You guide your people to springs of the water
of life. We pray for the church in all places,
that we may know the freedom of life in the
Spirit.
(open prayers)
You bless those who mourn;
they will be comforted.

Your glory will shine over all the earth and
sea. We pray for the world and for all who
care for creation.
(open prayers)
You bless those who mourn;
they will be comforted.

We offer you other concerns we carry in our
hearts.
(open prayers)
You bless those who mourn;
they will be comforted.

God of compassion and joy,
you satisfy all who hunger
for your righteousness.
Give us grace to endure testing

and be true to your kingdom,
that we may enjoy the life you bless.
Through Jesus,
who taught us to do so,
we pray for the coming of your reign:

Our Father ...

Benediction
May the Father of mercies
and the God of all comfort
comfort us in our affliction,
so that we may be able
to comfort those who are afflicted
with the consolation
with which we ourselves are consoled by God.
Amen.

Blessed are the meek

Opening sentence

Blessed are the meek,
for they will inherit the earth.

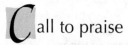all to praise

Lord, open our lips
and our mouths will proclaim your praise.
You are good to those who wait for you,
to all who seek you.

Glory ...

Psalm 37.3-11

If you trust in the LORD and do good,
then you will live in the land and be secure.
If you find your delight in the LORD,
he will grant your heart's desire.

Commit your life to the LORD,
be confident, and God will act,
so that your justice breaks forth like the light,
your cause like the noonday sun.

Be still before the LORD and wait in patience;
do not fret at those who prosper;

those who make evil plots
to bring down the needy and the poor.

Calm your anger and forget your rage;
do not fret, it only leads to evil.
For those who do evil shall perish;
those waiting for the LORD
shall inherit the land.

A little longer—
and the wicked shall have gone.
Look at their homes, they are not there.
But the humble shall own the land
and enjoy the fullness of peace.

Thanksgiving

My heart is ready, O God;
I will sing your praise.
Your steadfast love is higher than the heavens,
and your faithfulness reaches to the clouds.
(free prayers of thanksgiving)
Be exalted, O God, above the heavens,
and let your glory shine over all the earth.
Amen.

Song

God moves in a mysterious way (SJ104)
Asithi: Amen (Sing amen) (H64)
Confitemini Domino (Come and fill our
    hearts) (SJ59)

*C*all to discipleship

Jesus said, Let anyone with ears to hear listen.
You shall love the Lord your God
with all your heart, and with all your soul,
and with all your strength,
and with all your mind;
and your neighbor as yourself.
Do this, and you will live.
Lord Jesus, you have the words of eternal life.

Luke 14.7-11

When [Jesus] noticed how the guests chose
the places of honor, he told them a parable.
"When you are invited by someone to a wedding banquet, do not sit down at the place of
honor, in case someone more distinguished
than you has been invited by your host; and
the host who invited both of you may come
and say to you, 'Give this person your place,'
and then in disgrace you would start to take
the lowest place. But when you are invited, go
and sit down at the lowest place, so that when
your host comes, he may say to you, 'Friend,
move up higher'; then you will be honored
in the presence of all who sit at the table with
you. For all who exalt themselves will be
humbled, and those who humble themselves
will be exalted."

Colossians 3.12-14

As God's chosen ones, holy and beloved, clothe yourselves with compassion, kindness, humility, meekness, and patience. Bear with one another and, if anyone has a complaint against another, forgive each other; just as the Lord has forgiven you, so you also must forgive. Above all, clothe yourselves with love, which binds everything together in perfect harmony.

Silent or spoken reflection on the readings

Song

Beloved, God's chosen (SJ38)
Christ, who is in the form of God (H333)
Take, O take me as I am (SJ81)

The Beatitudes

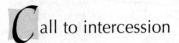

Call to intercession

Rejoice in the Lord always.
The Lord is near.
Do not worry about anything,
but in everything with thanksgiving
let your requests be made known to God.

God, guide of the humble, we bring our prayers to you as acts of love for you and for our neighbors.
In your mercy, Lord, hear our prayer.

You call us to confidence and trust in you. We pray for ourselves and those dear to us.
(open prayers)
You bless the meek;
they will inherit the earth.

You exalt those who are humbled. We pray for our community and for our neighbors.
(open prayers)
You bless the meek;
they will inherit the earth.

You show the right path to those who revere your name. We pray for the church in all places, that we may reflect your faithful love.
(open prayers)
You bless the meek;
they will inherit the earth.

You offer the fullness of peace to the humble. We pray for the world, for those who are in need.
(open prayers)
You bless the meek;
they will inherit the earth.

We offer you other concerns we carry in our hearts.
(open prayers)
You bless the meek;
they will inherit the earth.

God whose justice shines like the sun,
you bless all who seek first
your kingdom and righteousness.
Fill our hearts
with the spirit of the Beatitudes,
that we may live this day
in simplicity, mercy, and joy.
Through Jesus,
who taught us to do so,
we pray for the coming of your reign:

Our Father ...

Benediction
Now to God,
who by the power at work within us
is able to accomplish abundantly
far more than all we can ask or imagine,
be glory in the church and in Christ Jesus
to all generations, forever and ever. Amen.

Blessed are the meek

WEEK 2 BEATITUDES

Opening sentence

Blessed are the meek,
for they will inherit the earth.

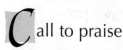all to praise

O God, your word is a lamp to my feet
and a light to my path.
The light and peace of Jesus Christ be with us.

Glory ...

Psalm 25.8-14

The LORD is good and upright,
showing the path to those who stray,
guiding the humble in the right path,
and teaching the way to the poor.

God's ways are steadfastness and truth
for those faithful to the covenant decrees.
LORD, for the sake of your name
forgive my guilt, for it is great.

Those who revere the LORD
will be shown the path they should choose.
Their souls will live in happiness
and their children shall possess the land.

The LORD's friendship is for the God-fearing;
and the covenant is revealed to them.

Thanksgiving

It is good to give thanks to the Lord,
to sing praises to your name, O Most High.
(free prayers of thanksgiving)
We declare your steadfast love in the morning,
and your faithfulness by night. Amen.

Song

Ehane he'ama (Father God, you are holy) (H78)
Make music to the Lord most high (H73)
I long for your commandments (H543)

Confession

Have mercy on me, O God,
according to your steadfast love;
according to your abundant mercy
blot out my transgressions.
(silence)
Create in me a clean heart, O God,
and put a new and right spirit within me.
Restore to me the joy of your salvation
and sustain in me a willing spirit. Amen.

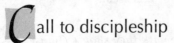

Call to discipleship

Jesus said, I am the bread of life.
Whoever comes to me will never be hungry,

and whoever believes in me
will never be thirsty.
Lord Jesus, you have the words of eternal life.

Mark 9.33-37

Then [Jesus and his disciples] came to
Capernaum; and when he was in the house he
asked them, "What were you arguing about
on the way?" But they were silent, for on the
way they had argued with one another who
was the greatest. He sat down, called the
twelve, and said to them, "Whoever wants to
be first must be last of all and servant of all."
Then he took a little child and put it among
them; and taking it in his arms, he said to
them, "Whoever welcomes one such child in
my name welcomes me, and whoever welcomes me welcomes not me but the one who
sent me."

Ephesians 4.1-3

I therefore, the prisoner in the Lord, beg you
to lead a life worthy of the calling to which
you have been called, with all humility and
gentleness, with patience, bearing with one
another in love, making every effort to maintain the unity of the Spirit in the bond of
peace.

Silent or spoken reflection on the readings

Song

Day by day, dear Lord (H569)
Will you let me be your servant (H307)
Help us to help each other (H362)

The Beatitudes

*C*all to intercession

Ask, and it will be given you;
search, and you will find;
knock, and the door will be opened for you.
The heavenly Father will give the Holy Spirit
to those who ask.

God, guide of the humble, we bring our
prayers to you with confidence, in the name
of our Lord Jesus.
In your mercy, Lord, hear our prayer.

You call us to confidence and trust in you. We
pray for ourselves and those dear to us.
(open prayers)
You bless the meek;
they will inherit the earth.

You exalt those who are humbled. We pray for
our community and for our neighbors.
(open prayers)
You bless the meek;
they will inherit the earth.

You show the right path to those who revere
your name. We pray for the church in all
places, that we may reflect your faithful love.
(open prayers)
You bless the meek;
they will inherit the earth.

You offer the fullness of peace to the humble.
We pray for the world, for those who are in
need.
(open prayers)
You bless the meek;
they will inherit the earth.

We offer you other concerns we carry in our
hearts.
(open prayers)
You bless the meek;
they will inherit the earth.

God of compassion and joy,
you satisfy all who hunger
for your righteousness.
Give us grace to endure testing
and be true to your kingdom,
that we may enjoy the life you bless.
Through Jesus,
who taught us to do so,
we pray for the coming of your reign:

Our Father ...

Benediction

Now to God,
who by the power at work within us
is able to accomplish abundantly
far more than all we can ask or imagine,
be glory in the church and in Christ Jesus
to all generations, forever and ever. Amen.

Blessed are those who hunger and thirst for righteousness

WEEK 2 BEATITUDES

Opening sentence

Blessed are those who hunger and thirst
for righteousness,
for they will be filled.

*C*all to praise

Lord, open our lips
and our mouths will proclaim your praise.
You are good to those who wait for you,
to all who seek you.

Glory ...

Psalm 36.6-10 [5-9]

Your love, LORD, reaches to heaven,
your truth to the skies.
Your justice is like God's mountain,
your judgments like the deep.

To mortals and beasts you give protection.
O LORD, how precious is your love.
My God, the children of the earth
find refuge in the shelter of your wings.

They feast on the riches of your house;
they drink from the stream of your delight.
In you is the source of life
and in your light we see light.

Thanksgiving

My heart is ready, O God;
I will sing your praise.
Your steadfast love is higher than the heavens,
and your faithfulness reaches to the clouds.
(*free prayers of thanksgiving*)
Be exalted, O God, above the heavens,
and let your glory shine over all the earth.
Amen.

Song

Immortal, invisible, God only wise (H70)
How wondrous great (H126)
Por la mañana (At break of day) (H647)

Call to discipleship

Jesus said, Let anyone with ears to hear listen.
You shall love the Lord your God
with all your heart, and with all your soul,
and with all your strength,
and with all your mind;
and your neighbor as yourself.
Do this, and you will live.
Lord Jesus, you have the words of eternal life.

Luke 19.1-10

[Jesus] entered Jericho and was passing
through it. A man was there named Zacchaeus;
he was a chief tax collector and was rich.
He was trying to see who Jesus was, but on
account of the crowd he could not, because
he was short in stature. So he ran ahead and
climbed a sycamore tree to see him, because
he was going to pass that way. When Jesus
came to the place, he looked up and said to
him, "Zacchaeus, hurry and come down; for
I must stay at your house today." So he hur-
ried down and was happy to welcome him.
All who saw it began to grumble and said,
"He has gone to be the guest of one who is a
sinner." Zacchaeus stood there and said to the
Lord, "Look, half of my possessions, Lord, I
will give to the poor; and if I have defrauded
anyone of anything, I will pay back four times
as much." Then Jesus said to him, "Today salvation has come to this house, because he too
is a son of Abraham. For the Son of Man came
to seek out and to save the lost."

Micah 6.6-8

"With what shall I come before the LORD,
and bow myself before God on high?
Shall I come before him with burnt offerings,
with calves a year old?

Will the LORD be pleased with thousands of
    rams,
with ten thousands of rivers of oil?
Shall I give my firstborn for my transgression,
the fruit of my body for the sin of my soul?"
He has told you, O mortal, what is good;
and what does the LORD require of you
but to do justice, and to love kindness,
and to walk humbly with your God?"

Silent or spoken reflection on the readings

Song
Heart and mind, possessions, Lord (H392)
What does the Lord require (H409/SS54)
Blessed are they (SS41)

The Beatitudes

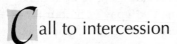

*C*all to intercession

Rejoice in the Lord always.
The Lord is near.
Do not worry about anything,
but in everything with thanksgiving
let your requests be made known to God.

Righteous God, we bring our prayers to you
as acts of love for you and for our neighbors.
In your mercy, Lord, hear our prayer.

You place in us the hunger and thirst for all that is right and good. We pray for ourselves and those dear to us.
(open prayers)
You bless those who hunger and thirst
for righteousness;
they will be filled.

You offer the refuge of your wings to the children of the earth. We pray for our community and for our neighbors.
(open prayers)
You bless those who hunger and thirst
for righteousness;
they will be filled.

You call us to love kindness and to walk humbly before you. We pray for the church in all places, that we may bear witness to your reign of justice, peace, and joy.
(open prayers)
You bless those who hunger and thirst
for righteousness;
they will be filled.

You come to rule the world with justice and truth. We pray for the world, for all who are ensnared in greed, violence, and oppression.
(open prayers)

You bless those who hunger and thirst
for righteousness;
they will be filled.

We offer you other concerns we carry in our
hearts.
(open prayers)
You bless those who hunger and thirst
for righteousness;
they will be filled.

God whose justice shines like the sun,
you bless all who seek first
your kingdom and righteousness.
Fill our hearts
with the spirit of the Beatitudes,
that we may live this day
in simplicity, mercy, and joy.
Through Jesus,
who taught us to do so,
we pray for the coming of your reign:

Our Father ...

Benediction
*May God, who supplies seed to the sower
and bread for food,
supply and multiply our seed for sowing
and increase the harvest of our righteousness.
Amen.*

Blessed are those who hunger and thirst for righteousness

WEEK 2 BEATITUDES

Opening sentence

Blessed are those who hunger and thirst
for righteousness,
for they will be filled.

*C*all to praise

O God, your word is a lamp to my feet
and a light to my path.
The light and peace of Jesus Christ be with us.

Glory ...

Psalm 96.10-13

Proclaim to the nations: "God is king."
The world was made firm in its place;
God will judge the people in fairness.

Let the heavens rejoice and earth be glad,
let the sea and all within it thunder praise,
let the land and all it bears rejoice,
all the trees of the wood shout for joy

at the presence of the LORD who comes,
who comes to rule the earth,

> *comes with justice to rule the world,*
> *and to judge the peoples with truth.*

Thanksgiving

It is good to give thanks to the Lord,
to sing praises to your name, O Most High.
(free prayers of thanksgiving)
We declare your steadfast love in the morning,
and your faithfulness by night. Amen.

Song

Let the heavens be glad (H187)
Joy to the world (H318)
Praise the Lord who reigns above (H54)

Confession

Have mercy on me, O God,
according to your steadfast love;
according to your abundant mercy
blot out my transgressions.
(silence)
Create in me a clean heart, O God,
and put a new and right spirit within me.
Restore to me the joy of your salvation
and sustain in me a willing spirit. Amen.

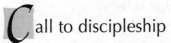# Call to discipleship

Jesus said, I am the bread of life.
Whoever comes to me will never be hungry,

and whoever believes in me
will never be thirsty.
Lord Jesus, you have the words of eternal life.

Matthew 5.20, 46-48

"For I tell you, unless your righteousness
exceeds that of the scribes and Pharisees, you
will never enter the kingdom of heaven.

"For if you love those who love you, what
reward do you have? Do not even the tax col-
lectors do the same? And if you greet only
your brothers and sisters, what more are you
doing than others? Do not even the Gentiles
do the same? Be perfect, therefore, as your
heavenly Father is perfect."

Amos 5.24

But let justice roll down like waters,
and righteousness like an everflowing stream.

Silent or spoken reflection on the readings

Song

O healing river (H372)
Rain down (SJ49)
Lord, I am fondly, earnestly (H514)

The Beatitudes

Call to intercession

Ask, and it will be given you;
search, and you will find;
knock, and the door will be opened for you.
*The heavenly Father will give the Holy Spirit
to those who ask.*

Righteous God, we bring our prayers to you
with confidence, in the name of our Lord
Jesus.
In your mercy, Lord, hear our prayer.

You place in us the hunger and thirst for all
that is right and good. We pray for ourselves
and those dear to us.
(open prayers)
You bless those who hunger and thirst
for righteousness;
they will be filled.

You offer the refuge of your wings to the
children of the earth. We pray for our
community and for our neighbors.
(open prayers)
You bless those who hunger and thirst
for righteousness;
they will be filled.

You call us to love kindness and to walk
humbly before you. We pray for the church in

all places, that we may bear witness to your reign of justice, peace, and joy.
(open prayers)
You bless those who hunger and thirst
for righteousness;
they will be filled.

You come to rule the world with justice and truth. We pray for the world, for all who are ensnared in greed, violence, and oppression.
(open prayers)
You bless those who hunger and thirst
for righteousness;
they will be filled.

We offer you other concerns we carry in our hearts.
(open prayers)
You bless those who hunger and thirst
for righteousness;
they will be filled.

God of compassion and joy,
you satisfy all who hunger
for your righteousness.
Give us grace to endure testing
and be true to your kingdom,
that we may enjoy the life you bless.
Through Jesus,
who taught us to do so,
we pray for the coming of your reign:

Our Father ...

Benediction
May God, who supplies seed to the sower
and bread for food,
supply and multiply our seed for sowing
and increase the harvest of our righteousness.
Amen.

Blessed are the merciful

WEEK 2 BEATITUDES

Opening sentence

Blessed are the merciful,
for they will receive mercy.

Call to praise

Lord, open our lips
and our mouths will proclaim your praise.
You are good to those who wait for you,
to all who seek you.

Glory …

Psalm 86.1-8

Turn your ear, O LORD, and give answer
for I am poor and needy.
Preserve my life, for I am faithful;
save the servant who trusts in you.

You are my God, have mercy on me, Lord,
for I cry to you all the day long.
Give joy to your servant, O Lord,
for to you I lift up my soul.

O Lord, you are good and forgiving,
full of love to all who call.

Give heed, O Lord, to my prayer
and attend to the sound of my voice.

In the day of distress I will call
and surely you will reply.
Among the gods
there is none like you, O Lord,
nor work to compare with yours.

Thanksgiving

My heart is ready, O God;
I will sing your praise.
Your steadfast love is higher than the heavens,
and your faithfulness reaches to the clouds.
(free prayers of thanksgiving)
Be exalted, O God, above the heavens,
and let your glory shine over all the earth.
Amen.

Song

My soul is filled with joy (SJ13)
What mercy and divine compassion (H524)
Come, thou fount (H521)

Call to discipleship

Jesus said, Let anyone with ears to hear listen.
You shall love the Lord your God
with all your heart, and with all your soul,
and with all your strength,

and with all your mind;
and your neighbor as yourself.
Do this, and you will live.
Lord Jesus, you have the words of eternal life.

Luke 6.32-38

"If you love those who love you, what credit
is that to you? For even sinners love those
who love them. If you do good to those who
do good to you, what credit is that to you?
For even sinners do the same. If you lend to
those from whom you hope to receive, what
credit is that to you? Even sinners lend to sinners, to receive as much again. But love your
enemies, do good, and lend, expecting nothing in return. Your reward will be great, and
you will be children of the Most High; for he
is kind to the ungrateful and the wicked. Be
merciful, just as your Father is merciful.

"Do not judge, and you will not be judged;
do not condemn, and you will not be con-
demned. Forgive, and you will be forgiven;
give, and it will be given to you. A good
measure, pressed down, shaken together, running over, will be put into your lap; for the
measure you give will be the measure you get
back."

Romans 12.9-16, (17-21)

Let love be genuine; hate what is evil, hold
fast to what is good; love one another with
mutual affection; outdo one another in showing honor. Do not lag in zeal, be ardent in
spirit, serve the Lord. Rejoice in hope, be
patient in suffering, persevere in prayer.
Contribute to the needs of the saints; extend
hospitality to strangers.

Bless those who persecute you; bless and
do not curse them. Rejoice with those who
rejoice, weep with those who weep. Live in
harmony with one another; do not be haughty,
but associate with the lowly; do not claim to
be wiser than you are.

Silent or spoken reflection on the readings

Song

Miren qué bueno (Behold, how pleasant) (SJ37)
Christ's is the world (SJ62)
How good a thing it is (H310)

The Beatitudes

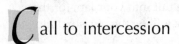 all to intercession

Rejoice in the Lord always.
The Lord is near.

Do not worry about anything,
but in everything with thanksgiving
let your requests be made known to God.

God, rich in mercy, we bring our prayers
to you as acts of love for you and for our
neighbors.
In your mercy, Lord, hear our prayer.

You have mercy on all who cry to you. We
pray for ourselves and those dear to us.
(open prayers)
You bless the merciful;
they will receive mercy.

You reveal yourself to the pure in heart.
We pray for our community and for our
neighbors.
(open prayers)
You bless the merciful;
they will receive mercy.

We long to stand in your holy place. We pray
for the church in all places, that we may daily
follow in the footsteps of Christ.
(open prayers)
You bless the merciful;
they will receive mercy.

You rule the earth in all its fullness. We pray
for the world, for those in positions of power
and authority.

(open prayers)
You bless the merciful;
they will receive mercy.

We offer you other concerns we carry in our
hearts.
(open prayers)
You bless the merciful;
they will receive mercy.

God whose justice shines like the sun,
you bless all who seek first
your kingdom and righteousness.
Fill our hearts
with the spirit of the Beatitudes,
that we may live this day
in simplicity, mercy, and joy.
Through Jesus,
who taught us to do so,
we pray for the coming of your reign:

Our Father ...

Benediction
By the tender mercy of our God,
the dawn from on high will break upon us
to give light to those who sit in darkness
and in the shadow of death,
to guide our feet into the way of peace. Amen.

Blessed are the pure in heart

WEEK 2 BEATITUDES

Opening sentence

Blessed are the pure in heart,
for they will see God.

*C*all to praise

O God, your word is a lamp to my feet
and a light to my path.
The light and peace of Jesus Christ be with us.

Glory ...

Psalm 24.1-6

The LORD's is the earth and its fullness,
the world and all its peoples.
It is God who set it on the seas;
who made it firm on the waters.

Who shall climb the mountain of the LORD?
Who shall stand in God's holy place?
Those with clean hands and pure heart,
who desire not worthless things,
(who have not sworn so as to deceive their
  neighbor.)

They shall receive blessings from the LORD
and reward from the God who saves them.

These are the ones who seek,
seek the face of the God of Jacob.

Thanksgiving

It is good to give thanks to the Lord,
to sing praises to your name, O Most High.
(free prayers of thanksgiving)
We declare your steadfast love in the morning,
and your faithfulness by night. Amen.

Song

Lord, our Lord, your glorious name (H157)
O come, loud anthems let us sing (H68)
From all that dwell below the skies (H49)

Confession

Have mercy on me, O God,
according to your steadfast love;
according to your abundant mercy
blot out my transgressions.
(silence)
Create in me a clean heart, O God,
and put a new and right spirit within me.
Restore to me the joy of your salvation
and sustain in me a willing spirit. Amen.

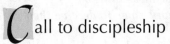Call to discipleship

Jesus said, I am the bread of life.
Whoever comes to me will never be hungry,

and whoever believes in me
will never be thirsty.
Lord Jesus, you have the words of eternal life.

John 1.47-51

When Jesus saw Nathanael coming toward
him, he said of him, "Here is truly an Israelite
in whom there is no deceit!" Nathanael
asked him, "Where did you get to know
me?" Jesus answered, "I saw you under the
fig tree before Philip called you." Nathanael
replied, "Rabbi, you are the Son of God! You
are the King of Israel!" Jesus answered, "Do
you believe because I told you that I saw you
under the fig tree? You will see greater things
than these." And he said to him, "Very truly,
I tell you, you will see heaven opened and
the angels of God ascending and descending
upon the Son of Man."

James 3.13-18

Who is wise and understanding among you?
Show by your good life that your works are
done with gentleness born of wisdom. But if
you have bitter envy and selfish ambition in
your hearts, do not be boastful and false to the
truth. Such wisdom does not come down from
above, but is earthly, unspiritual, devilish.
For where there is envy and selfish ambition,
there will also be disorder and wickedness of

every kind. But the wisdom from above is first pure, then peaceable, gentle, willing to yield, full of mercy and good fruits, without a trace of partiality or hypocrisy. And a harvest of righteousness is sown in peace for those who make peace.

Silent or spoken reflection on the readings

Song

Heart with loving heart united (H420)
We are people of God's peace (H407)
Ubi Caritas (Where true love) (SJ39)

The Beatitudes

*C*all to intercession

Ask, and it will be given you;
search, and you will find;
knock, and the door will be opened for you.
The heavenly Father will give the Holy Spirit to those who ask.

God, rich in mercy, we bring our prayers to you with confidence, in the name of our Lord Jesus.
In your mercy, Lord, hear our prayer.

You have mercy on all who cry to you. We pray for ourselves and those dear to us.

(open prayers)
You bless the pure in heart;
they will see you.

You reveal yourself to the pure in heart.
We pray for our community and for our
neighbors.
(open prayers)
You bless the pure in heart;
they will see you.

We long to stand in your holy place. We pray
for the church in all places, that we may daily
follow in the footsteps of Christ.
(open prayers)
You bless the pure in heart;
they will see you.

You rule the earth in all its fullness. We pray
for the world, for those in positions of power
and authority.
(open prayers)
You bless the pure in heart;
they will see you.

We offer you other concerns we carry in our
hearts.
(open prayers)
You bless the pure in heart;
they will see you.

God of compassion and joy,
you satisfy all who hunger
for your righteousness.
Give us grace to endure testing
and be true to your kingdom,
that we may enjoy the life you bless.
Through Jesus,
who taught us to do so,
we pray for the coming of your reign:

Our Father ...

Benediction

By the tender mercy of our God,
the dawn from on high will break upon us,
to give light to those who sit in darkness
and in the shadow of death,
to guide our feet into the way of peace. Amen.

Blessed are the peacemakers

Opening sentence

Blessed are the peacemakers,
for they will be called children of God.

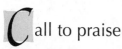all to praise

Lord, open our lips
and our mouths will proclaim your praise.
You are good to those who wait for you,
to all who seek you.

Glory ...

Psalm 85.8-14 [7-13]

Let us see, O LORD, your mercy
and give us your saving help.

I will hear what the LORD has to say,
a voice that speaks of peace,
peace for his people and friends
and those who turn to God in their hearts.
Salvation is near for the God-fearing,
and his glory will dwell in our land.

Mercy and faithfulness have met;
justice and peace have embraced.

Faithfulness shall spring from the earth
and justice look down from heaven.

The LORD will make us prosper
and our earth shall yield its fruit.
Justice shall march in the forefront,
and peace shall follow the way.

Thanksgiving

My heart is ready, O God;
I will sing your praise.
Your steadfast love is higher than the heavens,
and your faithfulness reaches to the clouds.
(free prayers of thanksgiving)
Be exalted, O God, above the heavens,
and let your glory shine over all the earth.
Amen.

Song

Praise with joy the world's Creator (SJ16)
He came down (SJ31)
God is here among us (H16)

Call to discipleship

Jesus said, Let anyone with ears to hear listen.
You shall love the Lord your God
with all your heart, and with all your soul,
and with all your strength,

and with all your mind;
and your neighbor as yourself.
Do this, and you will live.
Lord Jesus, you have the words of eternal life.

Matthew 5.38-45

"You have heard that it was said, 'An eye for
an eye and a tooth for a tooth.' But I say to
you, Do not resist an evildoer. But if anyone
strikes you on the right cheek, turn the other
also; and if anyone wants to sue you and
take your coat, give your cloak as well; and if
anyone forces you to go one mile, go also the
second mile. Give to everyone who begs from
you, and do not refuse anyone who wants to
borrow from you.

"You have heard that it was said, 'You shall
love your neighbor and hate your enemy.' But
I say to you, Love your enemies and pray for
those who persecute you, so that you may
be children of your Father in heaven; for he
makes his sun rise on the evil and on the
good, and sends rain on the righteous and on
the unrighteous."

Ephesians 2.14-18, (19-22)

For [Christ] is our peace; in his flesh he has
made both groups into one and has broken
down the dividing wall, that is, the hostility
between us. He has abolished the law with

its commandments and ordinances, that he might create in himself one new humanity in place of the two, thus making peace, and might reconcile both groups to God in one body through the cross, thus putting to death that hostility through it. So he came and proclaimed peace to you who were far off and peace to those who were near; for through him both of us have access in one Spirit to the Father.

Silent or spoken reflection on the readings

Song

And is the gospel peace and love (H406)
We shall walk through the valley (H412)
God of the Bible (SJ27)

The Beatitudes

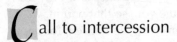

*C*all to intercession

Rejoice in the Lord always.
The Lord is near.
Do not worry about anything,
but in everything with thanksgiving
let your requests be made known to God.

God, breaker of dividing walls, we bring our prayers to you as acts of love for you and for our neighbors.
In your mercy, Lord, hear our prayer.

You are good and forgiving, full of love to all who call. We pray for ourselves and those dear to us.
(open prayers)
You bless the peacemakers;
they will be called your children.

Your generosity is impartial. We pray for our community and for our neighbors.
(open prayers)
You bless the peacemakers;
they will be called your children.

You proclaim peace to those who turn to you in their hearts. We pray for the church in all places, that we may speak boldly for Christ.
(open prayers)
You bless the peacemakers;
they will be called your children.

Your justice will march, and peace will follow the way. We pray for the world, for all who do justice and love mercy.
(open prayers)
You bless the peacemakers;
they will be called your children.

We offer you other concerns we carry in our hearts.
(open prayers)
You bless the peacemakers;
they will be called your children.

God whose justice shines like the sun,
you bless all who seek first
your kingdom and righteousness.
Fill our hearts
with the spirit of the Beatitudes,
that we may live this day
in simplicity, mercy, and joy.
Through Jesus,
who taught us to do so,
we pray for the coming of your reign:

Our Father …

Benediction
May the God of peace sanctify us entirely;
and may our spirit and soul and body
be kept sound and blameless
at the coming of our Lord Jesus Christ.
The one who calls us is faithful
and will do this. Amen.

Blessed are the peacemakers

Opening sentence

Blessed are the peacemakers,
for they will be called children of God.

*C*all to praise

O God, your word is a lamp to my feet
and a light to my path.
The light and peace of Jesus Christ be with us.

Glory ...

Psalm 34.12-19 [11-18]

Come, children, and hear me
that I may teach you the fear of the Lord.
Who are those who long for life
and many days, to enjoy their prosperity?

Then keep your tongue from evil
and your lips from speaking deceit.
Turn aside from evil and do good;
seek and strive after peace.

The eyes of the Lord are toward the just
and his ears toward their appeal.
The face of the Lord rebuffs the wicked
to destroy their remembrance from the earth.

They call and the LORD hears
and rescues them in all their distress.
The LORD is close to the broken-hearted;
those whose spirit is crushed God will save.

Thanksgiving

It is good to give thanks to the Lord,
to sing praises to your name, O Most High.
(free prayers of thanksgiving)
We declare your steadfast love in the morning,
and your faithfulness by night. Amen.

Song

Bless'd be the God of Israel (H174)
I'll praise my Maker (H166)
O Holy Spirit, Root of life (H123)

Confession

Have mercy on me, O God,
according to your steadfast love;
according to your abundant mercy
blot out my transgressions.
(silence)
Create in me a clean heart, O God,
and put a new and right spirit within me.
Restore to me the joy of your salvation
and sustain in me a willing spirit. Amen.

*C*all to discipleship

Jesus said, I am the bread of life.
Whoever comes to me will never be hungry,
and whoever believes in me
will never be thirsty.
Lord Jesus, you have the words of eternal life.

John 14.25-27

"I have said these things to you while I am
still with you. But the Advocate, the Holy
Spirit, whom the Father will send in my name,
will teach you everything, and remind you of
all that I have said to you. Peace I leave with
you; my peace I give to you. I do not give to
you as the world gives. Do not let your hearts
be troubled, and do not let them be afraid."

Isaiah 32.15-18

A spirit from on high is poured out on us,
and the wilderness becomes a fruitful field,
and the fruitful field is deemed a forest.
Then justice will dwell in the wilderness,
and righteousness abide in the fruitful field.
The effect of righteousness will be peace,
and the result of righteousness, quietness and
  trust forever.
My people will abide in a peaceful habitation,
in secure dwellings, and in quiet resting
  places.

Silent or spoken reflection on the readings

Song

The God of Abraham praise (H162)
O Holy Spirit, by whose breath (H291)
God sends us the Spirit (H293)

The Beatitudes

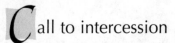

Call to intercession

Ask, and it will be given you;
search, and you will find;
knock, and the door will be opened for you.
***The heavenly Father will give the Holy Spirit
to those who ask.***

God, breaker of dividing walls, we bring our
prayers to you with confidence, in the name
of our Lord Jesus.
In your mercy, Lord, hear our prayer.

You are good and forgiving, full of love to
all who call. We pray for ourselves and those
dear to us.
(open prayers)
You bless the peacemakers;
they will be called your children.

Your generosity is impartial. We pray for our
community and for our neighbors.

(open prayers)
You bless the peacemakers;
they will be called your children.

You proclaim peace to those who turn to you
in their hearts. We pray for the church in all
places, that we may speak boldly for Christ.
(open prayers)
You bless the peacemakers;
they will be called your children.

Your justice will march, and peace will follow
the way. We pray for the world, for all who do
justice and love mercy.
(open prayers)
You bless the peacemakers;
they will be called your children.

We offer you other concerns we carry in our
hearts.
(open prayers)
You bless the peacemakers;
they will be called your children.

God of compassion and joy,
you satisfy all who hunger
for your righteousness.
Give us grace to endure testing
and be true to your kingdom,
that we may enjoy the life you bless.
Through Jesus,

who taught us to do so,
we pray for the coming of your reign:

Our Father …

Benediction
May the Lord bless us and keep us.
May the face of God shine on us
and be gracious to us.
May God's presence embrace us
and give us peace. Amen.

Blessed are those
who are persecuted

WEEK 2 BEATITUDES

Opening sentence

Blessed are those who are persecuted
for righteousness' sake,
for theirs is the kingdom of heaven.

Call to praise

Lord, open our lips
and our mouths will proclaim your praise.
You are good to those who wait for you,
to all who seek you.

Glory …

Psalm 31.20-25 [19-24]

How great is the goodness, LORD,
that you keep for those who fear you,
*that you show to those who trust you
in the sight of all.*

You hide them in the shelter of your presence
from human plots;
*you keep them safe within your tent
from disputing tongues.*

Blessed be the LORD who has shown me
such a steadfast love
in a fortified city.

"I am far removed from your sight,"
I said in my alarm.
Yet you heard the voice of my plea
when I cried for help.

Love the LORD, all you saints.
The LORD guards the faithful
but in turn will repay to the full
those who act with pride.

Be strong, let your heart take courage,
all who hope in the LORD.

Thanksgiving

My heart is ready, O God;
I will sing your praise.
Your steadfast love is higher than the heavens,
and your faithfulness reaches to the clouds.
(free prayers of thanksgiving)
Be exalted, O God, above the heavens,
and let your glory shine over all the earth.
Amen.

Song

All glory be to God on high (H122)
To God, with the Lamb (H125)
Alleluia (SS87)

*C*all to discipleship

Jesus said, Let anyone with ears to hear listen.
You shall love the Lord your God
with all your heart, and with all your soul,
and with all your strength,
and with all your mind;
and your neighbor as yourself.
Do this, and you will live.
Lord Jesus, you have the words of eternal life.

John 15.18-20

"If the world hates you, be aware that it hated
me before it hated you. If you belonged to the
world, the world would love you as its own.
Because you do not belong to the world, but I
have chosen you out of the world—therefore
the world hates you. Remember the word that
I said to you, 'Servants are not greater than
their master.' If they persecuted me, they will
persecute you; if they kept my word, they will
keep yours also."

2 Timothy 1.7-10

For God did not give us a spirit of cowardice,
but rather a spirit of power and of love and of
self-discipline.

Do not be ashamed, then, of the testimony
about our Lord or of me his prisoner, but join

with me in suffering for the gospel, relying on the power of God, who saved us and called us with a holy calling, not according to our works but according to his own purpose and grace. This grace was given to us in Christ Jesus before the ages began, but it has now been revealed through the appearing of our Savior Christ Jesus, who abolished death and brought life and immortality to light through the gospel.

Silent or spoken reflection on the readings

Song
Living and dying with Jesus (H550)
Lord, you give the great commission (SJ63)
Who now would follow Christ (H535)

The Beatitudes

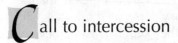 all to intercession

Rejoice in the Lord always.
The Lord is near.
Do not worry about anything,
but in everything with thanksgiving
let your requests be made known to God.

God of joy, we bring our prayers to you as
acts of love for you and for our neighbors.
In your mercy, Lord, hear our prayer.

You call us to take courage and to hope in you.
We pray for ourselves and those dear to us.
(open prayers)
You bless those who are persecuted
for righteousness' sake;
theirs is the kingdom of heaven.

You show goodness to those who trust you in
the sight of all. We pray for our community
and for our neighbors.
(open prayers)
You bless those who are persecuted
for righteousness' sake;
theirs is the kingdom of heaven.

You strengthen your people with wisdom. We
pray for the church in all places, that we may
be faithful in solidarity across generations and
geography.
(open prayers)
You bless those who are persecuted
for righteousness' sake;
theirs is the kingdom of heaven.

Yours is the Spirit of reconciling love and
healing power. We pray for the world, for our
enemies and for those who are in conflict.
(open prayers)

You bless those who are persecuted
for righteousness' sake;
theirs is the kingdom of heaven.

We offer you other concerns we carry in our
hearts.
(open prayers)
You bless those who are persecuted
for righteousness' sake;
theirs is the kingdom of heaven.

God whose justice shines like the sun,
you bless all who seek first
your kingdom and righteousness.
Fill our hearts
with the spirit of the Beatitudes,
that we may live this day
in simplicity, mercy, and joy.
Through Jesus,
who taught us to do so,
we pray for the coming of your reign:

Our Father …

Benediction
***And after we have suffered for a little while,
the God of all grace,
who has called us to eternal glory in Christ,
will restore, support, strengthen,
and establish us. Amen.***

Blessed are those
who are persecuted

WEEK 2 BEATITUDES

Opening sentence

Blessed are those who are persecuted
for righteousness' sake,
for theirs is the kingdom of heaven.

*C*all to praise

O God, your word is a lamp to my feet
and a light to my path.
The light and peace of Jesus Christ be with us.

Glory ...

Psalm 43

Defend me, O God, and plead my cause
against a godless nation.
*From a deceitful and cunning people
rescue me, O God.*

Since you, O God, are my stronghold,
why have you rejected me?
*Why do I go mourning
oppressed by the foe?*

O send forth your light and your truth;
let these be my guide.
Let them bring me to your holy mountain,
to the place where you dwell.

And I will come to your altar, O God,
the God of my joy.
My redeemer, I will thank you on the harp,
O God, my God.

Why are you cast down, my soul,
why groan within me?
Hope in God; I will praise yet again,
my savior and my God.

Thanksgiving

It is good to give thanks to the Lord,
to sing praises to your name, O Most High.
(free prayers of thanksgiving)
We declare your steadfast love in the morning,
and your faithfulness by night. Amen.

Song

God is our refuge and strength (SJ26)
Great is thy faithfulness (H327)
O Love of God (H326)

Confession

Have mercy on me, O God,
according to your steadfast love;
according to your abundant mercy
blot out my transgressions.

(silence)
Create in me a clean heart, O God,
and put a new and right spirit within me.
***Restore to me the joy of your salvation
and sustain in me a willing spirit. Amen.***

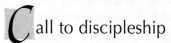all to discipleship

Jesus said, I am the bread of life.
Whoever comes to me will never be hungry,
and whoever believes in me
will never be thirsty.
Lord Jesus, you have the words of eternal life.

Matthew 10.16-20

"See, I am sending you out like sheep into the
midst of wolves; so be wise as serpents and
innocent as doves. Beware of them, for they
will hand you over to councils and flog you
in their synagogues; and you will be dragged
before governors and kings because of me, as
a testimony to them and the Gentiles. When
they hand you over, do not worry about how
you are to speak or what you are to say; for
what you are to say will be given to you at
that time; for it is not you who speak, but the
Spirit of your Father speaking through you."

1 Peter 3.13-16

Now who will harm you if you are eager to do what is good? But even if you do suffer for doing what is right, you are blessed. Do not fear what they fear, and do not be intimidated, but in your hearts sanctify Christ as Lord. Always be ready to make your defense to anyone who demands from you an accounting for the hope that is in you; yet do it with gentleness and reverence. Keep your conscience clear, so that, when you are maligned, those who abuse you for your good conduct in Christ may be put to shame.

Silent or spoken reflection on the readings

Song

Take up your cross (H536)
Strong, righteous man of Galilee (H540)
How clear is our vocation, Lord (H541)

The Beatitudes

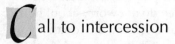

Call to intercession

Ask, and it will be given you;
search, and you will find;
knock, and the door will be opened for you.
***The heavenly Father will give the Holy Spirit
to those who ask.***

God of joy, we bring our prayers to you with confidence, in the name of our Lord Jesus.
In your mercy, Lord, hear our prayer.

You call us to take courage and to hope in you. We pray for ourselves and those dear to us.
(open prayers)
You bless those who are persecuted
for righteousness' sake;
theirs is the kingdom of heaven.

You show goodness to those who trust you in the sight of all. We pray for our community and for our neighbors.
(open prayers)
You bless those who are persecuted
for righteousness' sake;
theirs is the kingdom of heaven.

You strengthen your people with wisdom. We pray for the church in all places, that we may be faithful in solidarity across generations and geography.
(open prayers)
You bless those who are persecuted
for righteousness' sake;
theirs is the kingdom of heaven.

Yours is the Spirit of reconciling love and healing power. We pray for the world, for our enemies and for those who are in conflict.
(open prayers)

You bless those who are persecuted
for righteousness' sake;
theirs is the kingdom of heaven.

We offer you other concerns we carry in our
hearts.
(open prayers)
You bless those who are persecuted
for righteousness' sake;
theirs is the kingdom of heaven.

God of compassion and joy,
you satisfy all who hunger
for your righteousness.
Give us grace to endure testing
and be true to your kingdom,
that we may enjoy the life you bless.
Through Jesus, who taught us to do so,
we pray for the coming of your reign:

Our Father ...

Benediction

*And after we have suffered for a little while,
the God of all grace,
who has called us to eternal glory in Christ,
will restore, support, strengthen,
and establish us. Amen.*

WEEK 3

Parables

Give heed to my teaching

WEEK 3 PARABLES

Opening sentence

Give heed, my people, to my teaching;
turn your ear to the words of my mouth.

*C*all to praise

Lord, open our lips
and our mouths will proclaim your praise.
You are good to those who wait for you,
to all who seek you.

Glory ...

Psalm 32.1-5

Happy those whose offense is forgiven,
whose sin is remitted.
*O happy those to whom the Lord
imputes no guilt,
in whose spirit is no guile.*

I kept it secret and my frame was wasted.
I groaned all day long,
*for night and day your hand
was heavy upon me.*
Indeed my strength was dried up
as by the summer's heat.

But now I have acknowledged my sins;
my guilt I did not hide.
I said: "I will confess
my offense to the LORD."
And you, Lord, have forgiven
the guilt of my sin.

Thanksgiving

My heart is ready, O God;
I will sing your praise.
Your steadfast love is higher than the heavens,
and your faithfulness reaches to the clouds.
(free prayers of thanksgiving)
Be exalted, O God, above the heavens,
and let your glory shine over all the earth.
Amen.

Song

Holy, holy, holy (H120)
We praise thee, O God (H99)
Praise, my soul, the God of heaven (H63)

Call to discipleship

Jesus said, Let anyone with ears to hear listen.
You shall love the Lord your God
with all your heart, and with all your soul,
and with all your strength,
and with all your mind;
and your neighbor as yourself.

Do this, and you will live.
Lord Jesus, you have the words of eternal life.

Luke 15.11-19

Then Jesus said, "There was a man who had two sons. The younger of them said to his father, 'Father, give me the share of the property that will belong to me.' So he divided his property between them. A few days later the younger son gathered all he had and traveled to a distant country, and there he squandered his property in dissolute living. When he had spent everything, a severe famine took place throughout that country, and he began to be in need. So he went and hired himself out to one of the citizens of that country, who sent him to his fields to feed the pigs. He would gladly have filled himself with the pods that the pigs were eating; and no one gave him anything. But when he came to himself he said, 'How many of my father's hired hands have bread enough and to spare, but here I am dying of hunger! I will get up and go to my father, and I will say to him, "Father, I have sinned against heaven and before you; I am no longer worthy to be called your son; treat me like one of your hired hands."'"

Romans 5.6-11

For while we were still weak, at the right time Christ died for the ungodly. Indeed, rarely will anyone die for a righteous person—though perhaps for a good person someone might actually dare to die. But God proves his love for us in that while we still were sinners Christ died for us. Much more surely then, now that we have been justified by his blood, will we be saved through him from the wrath of God. For if while we were enemies, we were reconciled to God through the death of his Son, much more surely, having been reconciled, will we be saved by his life. But more than that, we even boast in God through our Lord Jesus Christ, through whom we have now received reconciliation.

Silent or spoken reflection on the readings

Song
Far, far away from my loving father (H139)
I know not why God's wondrous (H338)
Amazing grace (H143)

Zechariah's song

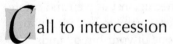

Call to intercession

Rejoice in the Lord always.
The Lord is near.

Do not worry about anything,
but in everything with thanksgiving
let your requests be made known to God.

God of forgiveness, we bring our prayers
to you as acts of love for you and for our
neighbors.
In your mercy, Lord, hear our prayer.

Your compassion reaches out to us. We pray
for ourselves and those dear to us.
(open prayers)
We come to you in times of need, O God;
hear our prayer.

Your love seeks even those who are far from
you. We pray for our community and for our
neighbors.
(open prayers)
We come to you in times of need, O God;
hear our prayer.

You are filled with compassion and long to
embrace all your children. We pray for the
church in all places, that we may be one.
(open prayers)
We come to you in times of need, O God;
hear our prayer.

You are rich in mercy toward all. We pray for
the world, that your reign may come and your
will be done on earth.

(open prayers)
We come to you in times of need, O God;
hear our prayer.

We offer you other concerns we carry in our
hearts.
(open prayers)
We come to you in times of need, O God;
hear our prayer.

God of surprises,
you sow your storied word in us
with compassion.
As this new day breaks upon us,
show us your mercy,
that we may extend it to others
and live for the sake of your reign.
In hope we pray:

Our Father ...

Benediction
Now may the God of peace,
who brought back from the dead
our Lord Jesus,
make us complete in everything good
so that we may do God's will,
through Jesus Christ,
to whom be the glory forever and ever. Amen.

Give heed to my teaching

Opening sentence

Give heed, my people, to my teaching;
turn your ear to the words of my mouth.

*C*all to praise

O God, your word is a lamp to my feet
and a light to my path.
The light and peace of Jesus Christ be with us.

Glory ...

Psalm 139.1-6

O LORD, you search me and you know me,
you know my resting and my rising,
you discern my purpose from afar.
You mark when I walk or lie down,
all my ways lie open to you.

Before ever a word is on my tongue
you know it, O LORD, through and through.
Behind and before you besiege me,
your hand ever laid upon me.
Too wonderful for me, this knowledge,
too high, beyond my reach.

Thanksgiving

It is good to give thanks to the Lord,
to sing praises to your name, O Most High.
(free prayers of thanksgiving)
We declare your steadfast love in the morning,
and your faithfulness by night. Amen.

Song

Santo (Holy) (SJ15)
I will praise the Lord (H109)
God is here among us (H16)

Confession

Have mercy on me, O God,
according to your steadfast love;
according to your abundant mercy
blot out my transgressions.
(silence)
Create in me a clean heart, O God,
and put a new and right spirit within me.
Restore to me the joy of your salvation
and sustain in me a willing spirit. Amen.

Call to discipleship

Jesus said, I am the bread of life.
Whoever comes to me will never be hungry,
and whoever believes in me
will never be thirsty.
Lord Jesus, you have the words of eternal life.

Luke 15.20-24

"[The younger son] set off and went to his father. But while he was still far off, his father saw him and was filled with compassion; he ran and put his arms around him and kissed him. Then the son said to him, 'Father, I have sinned against heaven and before you; I am no longer worthy to be called your son.' But the father said to his slaves, 'Quickly, bring out a robe—the best one—and put it on him; put a ring on his finger and sandals on his feet. And get the fatted calf and kill it, and let us eat and celebrate; for this son of mine was dead and is alive again; he was lost and is found!' And they began to celebrate."

Romans 8.35-39

Who will separate us from the love of Christ? Will hardship, or distress, or persecution, or famine, or nakedness, or peril, or sword? As it is written,

"For your sake we are being killed all day
    long;
we are accounted as sheep to be
    slaughtered."

No, in all these things we are more than conquerors through him who loved us. For I am convinced that neither death, nor life, nor angels, nor rulers, nor things present, nor things to come, nor powers, nor height, nor

depth, nor anything else in all creation, will
be able to separate us from the love of God in
Christ Jesus our Lord.

Silent or spoken reflection on the readings

Song
I sought the Lord (H506)
What wondrous love is this (H530)
Come, my Way, my Truth, my Life (H587)

Mary's *or* Simeon's song

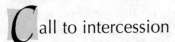

*C*all to intercession

Ask, and it will be given you;
search, and you will find;
knock, and the door will be opened for you.
***The heavenly Father will give the Holy Spirit
to those who ask.***

God of forgiveness, we bring our prayers to
you with confidence, in the name of our Lord
Jesus.
In your mercy, Lord, hear our prayer.

Your compassion reaches out to us. We pray
for ourselves and those dear to us.
(open prayers)
We come to you in times of need, O God;
hear our prayer.

Your love seeks even those who are far from you. We pray for our community and for our neighbors.
(open prayers)
We come to you in times of need, O God;
hear our prayer.

You are filled with compassion and long to embrace all your children. We pray for the church in all places, that we may be one.
(open prayers)
We come to you in times of need, O God;
hear our prayer.

You are rich in mercy toward all. We pray for the world, that your reign may come and your will be done on earth.
(open prayers)
We come to you in times of need, O God;
hear our prayer.

We offer you other concerns we carry in our hearts.
(open prayers)
We come to you in times of need, O God;
hear our prayer.

Generous God,
you draw us into surprising stories.
Use them to disrupt our complacency
and remove our fear,
that we may follow you

into the joy of your kingdom.
In the name of the one
who taught us not to lose heart, we pray:

Our Father ...

Benediction

Now may the God of peace,
who brought back from the dead
our Lord Jesus,
make us complete in everything good
so that we may do God's will,
through Jesus Christ,
to whom be the glory forever and ever. Amen.

Turn your ear to the words

Opening sentence

Give heed, my people, to my teaching;
turn your ear to the words of my mouth.

*C*all to praise

Lord, open our lips
and our mouths will proclaim your praise.
You are good to those who wait for you,
to all who seek you.

Glory ...

Psalm 65.10-14 [9-13]

You care for the earth, give it water;
you fill it with riches.
Your river in heaven brims over
to provide its grain.

And thus you provide for the earth;
you drench its furrows;
you level it, soften it with showers;
you bless its growth.

You crown the year with your goodness.
Abundance flows in your steps;
in the pastures of the wilderness it flows.

The hills are girded with joy,
the meadows covered with flocks,
the valleys are decked with wheat.
They shout for joy, yes, they sing.

Thanksgiving

My heart is ready, O God;
I will sing your praise.
Your steadfast love is higher than the heavens,
and your faithfulness reaches to the clouds.
(free prayers of thanksgiving)
Be exalted, O God, above the heavens,
and let your glory shine over all the earth.
Amen.

Song

For the fruit of all creation (H90)
Sing to the Lord of harvest (H98)
We plow the fields and scatter (H96)

Call to discipleship

Jesus said, Let anyone with ears to hear listen.
You shall love the Lord your God
with all your heart, and with all your soul,
and with all your strength,
and with all your mind;
and your neighbor as yourself.
Do this, and you will live.
Lord Jesus, you have the words of eternal life.

Mark 4.1-9

Again [Jesus] began to teach beside the sea. Such a very large crowd gathered around him that he got into a boat on the sea and sat there, while the whole crowd was beside the sea on the land. He began to teach them many things in parables, and in his teaching he said to them: "Listen! A sower went out to sow. And as he sowed, some seed fell on the path, and the birds came and ate it up. Other seed fell on rocky ground, where it did not have much soil, and it sprang up quickly, since it had no depth of soil. And when the sun rose, it was scorched; and since it had no root, it withered away. Other seed fell among thorns, and the thorns grew up and choked it, and it yielded no grain. Other seed fell into good soil and brought forth grain, growing up and increasing and yielding thirty and sixty and a hundredfold." And he said, "Let anyone with ears to hear listen!"

Colossians 1.9-12

For this reason, since the day we heard it, we have not ceased praying for you and asking that you may be filled with the knowledge of God's will in all spiritual wisdom and under-standing, so that you may lead lives worthy of the Lord, fully pleasing to him, as you bear fruit in every good work and as you grow in the knowledge of God. May you be made strong with all the strength that comes from his glorious power, and may you be prepared to endure everything with patience, while joyfully giving thanks to the Father, who has enabled you to share in the inheritance of the saints in the light.

Silent or spoken reflection on the readings

Song
God of the fertile fields (H390)
Take my life and let it be (H389)
Heart and mind, possessions, Lord (H392)

Zechariah's song

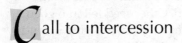

*C*all to intercession

Rejoice in the Lord always.
The Lord is near.
Do not worry about anything,
but in everything with thanksgiving
let your requests be made known to God.

God whose word is trustworthy, we bring our prayers to you as acts of love for you and for our neighbors.
In your mercy, Lord, hear our prayer.

You entrust the seed of your word to the soil
of our lives. We pray for ourselves and those
dear to us.
(open prayers)
You can do more than we ask
or imagine, Lord;
hear our prayer.

You accomplish your will through your word.
We pray for our community and for our
neighbors.
(open prayers)
You can do more than we ask
or imagine, Lord;
hear our prayer.

You multiply small acts of faithfulness. We
pray for the church in all places, that we may
know the freedom of life in the Spirit.
(open prayers)
You can do more than we ask
or imagine, Lord;
hear our prayer.

You delight in the beauty and bounty of your
creation. We pray for the world and for all
who care for creation.
(open prayers)
You can do more than we ask
or imagine, Lord;
hear our prayer.

We offer you other concerns we carry in our
hearts.
(open prayers)
You can do more than we ask
or imagine, Lord;
hear our prayer.

God of surprises,
you sow your storied word in us
with compassion.
As this day breaks upon us,
may we remember your mercy
and extend it to others
as we live for the sake of your reign.
In hope we pray:

Our Father ...

Benediction
The Lord will guide us continually,
and satisfy our needs in parched places,
and we shall be like a watered garden,
like a spring of water,
whose waters never fail. Amen.

Turn your ear to the words

WEEK 3 PARABLES

Opening sentence

Give heed, my people, to my teaching;
turn your ear to the words of my mouth.

Call to praise

O God, your word is a lamp to my feet
and a light to my path.
The light and peace of Jesus Christ be with us.

Glory ...

Psalm 19.8-10 [7-9]

The law of the LORD is perfect,
it revives the soul.
The rule of the LORD is to be trusted,
it gives wisdom to the simple.

The precepts of the LORD are right,
they gladden the heart.
The command of the LORD is clear,
it gives light to the eyes.

The fear of the LORD is holy,
abiding for ever.
The decrees of the LORD are truth
and all of them just.

Thanksgiving

It is good to give thanks to the Lord,
to sing praises to your name, O Most High.
(free prayers of thanksgiving)
We declare your steadfast love in the morning,
and your faithfulness by night. Amen.

Song

I long for your commandments (H543)
Lord, I have made thy word (H317)
Rejoice, rejoice in God (H313)

Confession

Have mercy on me, O God,
according to your steadfast love;
according to your abundant mercy
blot out my transgressions.
(silence)
Create in me a clean heart, O God,
and put a new and right spirit within me.
Restore to me the joy of your salvation
and sustain in me a willing spirit. Amen.

Call to discipleship

Jesus said, I am the bread of life.
Whoever comes to me will never be hungry,
and whoever believes in me
will never be thirsty.
Lord Jesus, you have the words of eternal life.

Luke 13.18-21

[Jesus] said therefore, "What is the kingdom of God like? And to what should I compare it? It is like a mustard seed that someone took and sowed in the garden; it grew and became a tree, and the birds of the air made nests in its branches."

And again he said, "To what should I compare the kingdom of God? It is like yeast that a woman took and mixed in with three measures of flour until all of it was leavened."

Ephesians 3.20-21

Now to [God] who by the power at work within us is able to accomplish abundantly far more than all we can ask or imagine, to him be glory in the church and in Christ Jesus to all generations, forever and ever. Amen.

Silent or spoken reflection on the readings

Song

The kingdom of God (H224)
Lord of light, your name outshining (H410)
O God, thou faithful God (H376)

Mary's *or* Simeon's song

*C*all to intercession

Ask, and it will be given you;
search, and you will find;
knock, and the door will be opened for you.
***The heavenly Father will give the Holy Spirit
to those who ask.***

God whose word is trustworthy, we bring our
prayers to you with confidence, in the name
of our Lord Jesus.
In your mercy, Lord, hear our prayer.

You entrust the seed of your word to the soil
of our lives. We pray for ourselves and those
dear to us.
(open prayers)
You can do more than we ask
or imagine, Lord;
hear our prayer.

You accomplish your will through your word.
We pray for our community and for our
neighbors.
(open prayers)
You can do more than we ask
or imagine, Lord;
hear our prayer.

You multiply small acts of faithfulness. We
pray for the church in all places, that we may
know the freedom of life in the Spirit.
(open prayers)
You can do more than we ask
or imagine, Lord;
hear our prayer.

You delight in the beauty and bounty of your
creation. We pray for the world and for all
who care for creation.
(open prayers)
You can do more than we ask
or imagine, Lord;
hear our prayer.

We offer you other concerns we carry in our
hearts.
(open prayers)
You can do more than we ask
or imagine, Lord;
hear our prayer.

Generous God,
you draw us into surprising stories.
Use them to disrupt our complacency
and remove our fear,
that we may follow you
into the joy of your kingdom.
In the name of the one
who taught us not to lose heart, we pray:

Our Father ...

Benediction
*May the God of hope fill us
with all joy and peace in believing
so that we may abound in hope
by the power of the Holy Spirit. Amen.*

I will open my mouth in a parable

WEEK 3 PARABLES

Opening sentence

Give heed, my people, to my teaching;
turn your ear to the words of my mouth.
I will open my mouth in a parable
and reveal hidden lessons of the past.

Call to praise

Lord, open our lips
and our mouths will proclaim your praise.
You are good to those who wait for you,
to all who seek you.

Glory ...

Psalm 51.14-19 [12-17]

Give me again the joy of your help;
with a spirit of fervor sustain me,
that I may teach transgressors your ways
and sinners may return to you.

O rescue me, God, my helper,
and my tongue shall ring out your goodness.
O Lord, open my lips
and my mouth shall declare your praise.

For in sacrifice you take no delight,
burnt offering from me you would refuse;
my sacrifice, a contrite spirit,
a humbled, contrite heart you will not spurn.

Thanksgiving

My heart is ready, O God;
I will sing your praise.
Your steadfast love is higher than the heavens,
and your faithfulness reaches to the clouds.
(free prayers of thanksgiving)
Be exalted, O God, above the heavens,
and let your glory shine over all the earth.
Amen.

Song

All glory be to God on high (H122)
Jesus, thou mighty Lord (H115)
What mercy and divine compassion (H524)

*C*all to discipleship

Jesus said, Let anyone with ears to hear listen.
You shall love the Lord your God
with all your heart, and with all your soul,
and with all your strength,
and with all your mind;
and your neighbor as yourself.
Do this, and you will live.
Lord Jesus, you have the words of eternal life.

Luke 18.9-14

[Jesus] also told this parable to some who trusted in themselves that they were righteous and regarded others with contempt: "Two men went up to the temple to pray, one a Pharisee and the other a tax collector. The Pharisee, standing by himself, was praying thus, 'God, I thank you that I am not like other people: thieves, rogues, adulterers, or even like this tax collector. I fast twice a week; I give a tenth of all my income.' But the tax collector, standing far off, would not even look up to heaven, but was beating his breast and saying, 'God, be merciful to me, a sinner!' I tell you, this man went down to his home justified rather than the other; for all who exalt themselves will be humbled, but all who humble themselves will be exalted."

1 Timothy 1.15-16

The saying is sure and worthy of full acceptance, that Christ Jesus came into the world to save sinners—of whom I am the foremost. But for that very reason I received mercy, so that in me, as the foremost, Jesus Christ might display the utmost patience, making me an example to those who would come to believe in him for eternal life.

Silent or spoken reflection on the readings

Song

The sacrifice you accept, O God (H141)
Let God, who called the worlds (H138)
Lord, I am fondly, earnestly (H514)

Zechariah's song

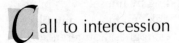

*C*all to intercession

Rejoice in the Lord always.
The Lord is near.
Do not worry about anything,
but in everything with thanksgiving
let your requests be made known to God.

God of boundless compassion, we bring our
prayers to you as acts of love for you and for
our neighbors.
In your mercy, Lord, hear our prayer.

You look on us with mercy and tenderness.
We pray for ourselves and those dear to us.
(open prayers)
Your word is faithful, Lord;
hear our prayer.

You are patient, waiting for all to turn to
you. We pray for our community and for our
neighbors.
(open prayers)

Your word is faithful, Lord;
hear our prayer.

You are compassionate, reaching out to all
who sin. We pray for the church in all places,
that we may reflect your faithful love.
(open prayers)
Your word is faithful, Lord;
hear our prayer.

You love justice and right. We pray for the
world, for those who are in need.
(open prayers)
Your word is faithful, Lord;
hear our prayer.

We offer you other concerns we carry in our
hearts.
(open prayers)
Your word is faithful, Lord;
hear our prayer.

God of surprises,
you sow your storied word in us
with compassion.
As this day breaks upon us,
may we remember your mercy
and extend it to others
as we live for the sake of your reign.
In hope we pray:

Our Father …

Benediction

*May we have all the riches
of assured understanding
and the knowledge of God's mystery,
that is, Christ himself. Amen.*

I will open my mouth in a parable

WEEK 3 PARABLES

Opening sentence

Give heed, my people, to my teaching;
turn your ear to the words of my mouth.
I will open my mouth in a parable
and reveal hidden lessons of the past.

Call to praise

O God, your word is a lamp to my feet
and a light to my path.
The light and peace of Jesus Christ be with us.

Glory ...

Psalm 33.1-5

Ring out your joy to the LORD, O you just;
for praise is fitting for loyal hearts.

Give thanks to the LORD upon the harp,
with a ten-stringed lute play your songs.
Sing to the Lord a song that is new,
play loudly, with all your skill.

For the word of the LORD is faithful
and all his works done in truth.
The LORD loves justice and right
and fills the earth with love.

Thanksgiving

It is good to give thanks to the Lord,
to sing praises to your name, O Most High.
(*free prayers of thanksgiving*)
We declare your steadfast love in the morning,
and your faithfulness by night. Amen.

Song

Praise with joy the world's Creator (SJ16)
Praise the Lord who reigns above (H54)
Earth and all stars (H47)

Confession

Have mercy on me, O God,
according to your steadfast love;
according to your abundant mercy
blot out my transgressions.
(*silence*)
Create in me a clean heart, O God,
and put a new and right spirit within me.
Restore to me the joy of your salvation
and sustain in me a willing spirit. Amen.

Call to discipleship

Jesus said, I am the bread of life.
Whoever comes to me will never be hungry,
and whoever believes in me
will never be thirsty.
Lord Jesus, you have the words of eternal life.

Luke 10.29-37

Wanting to justify himself, [the lawyer] asked Jesus, "And who is my neighbor?" Jesus replied, "A man was going down from Jerusalem to Jericho, and fell into the hands of robbers, who stripped him, beat him, and went away, leaving him half dead. Now by chance a priest was going down that road; and when he saw him, he passed by on the other side. So likewise a Levite, when he came to the place and saw him, passed by on the other side. But a Samaritan while traveling came near him; and when he saw him, he was moved with pity. He went to him and bandaged his wounds, having poured oil and wine on them. Then he put him on his own animal, brought him to an inn, and took care of him. The next day he took out two denarii, gave them to the innkeeper, and said, 'Take care of him; and when I come back, I will repay you whatever more you spend.' Which of these three, do you think, was a neighbor to the man who fell into the hands of the robbers?" He said, "The one who showed him mercy." Jesus said to him, "Go and do likewise."

James 2.8

You do well if you really fulfill the royal law according to the scripture, "You shall love your neighbor as yourself."

Silent or spoken reflection on the readings

Song

I bind my heart this tide (H411)
God, whose purpose is to kindle (H135)
Who has known the mind of Jesus? (SJ58)

Mary's *or* Simeon's song

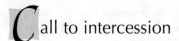

Call to intercession

Ask, and it will be given you;
search, and you will find;
knock, and the door will be opened for you.
***The heavenly Father will give the Holy Spirit
to those who ask.***

God of boundless compassion, we bring our prayers to you with confidence, in the name of our Lord Jesus.
In your mercy, Lord, hear our prayer.

You look on us with mercy and tenderness.
We pray for ourselves and those dear to us.
(open prayers)

Your word is faithful, Lord;
hear our prayer.

You are patient, waiting for all to turn to
you. We pray for our community and for our
neighbors.
(open prayers)
Your word is faithful, Lord;
hear our prayer.

You are compassionate, reaching out to all
who sin. We pray for the church in all places,
that we may reflect your faithful love.
(open prayers)
Your word is faithful, Lord;
hear our prayer.

You love justice and right. We pray for the
world, for those who are in need.
(open prayers)
Your word is faithful, Lord;
hear our prayer.

We offer you other concerns we carry in our
hearts.
(open prayers)
Your word is faithful, Lord;
hear our prayer.

Generous God,
you draw us into surprising stories.
Use them to disrupt our complacency

and remove our fear,
that we may follow you
into the joy of your kingdom.
In the name of the one
who taught us not to lose heart, we pray:

Our Father ...

Benediction
Let us abide in him,
so that when Christ is revealed
we may have confidence
and not be put to shame before him
at his coming. Amen.

Our ancestors have told us

Opening sentence

I will open my mouth in a parable
and reveal hidden lessons of the past.
The things we have heard and understood,
the things our ancestors have told us,
these we will not hide from their children.

*C*all to praise

Lord, open our lips
and our mouths will proclaim your praise.
You are good to those who wait for you,
to all who seek you.

Glory ...

Psalm 145.15-21

The eyes of all creatures look to you
and you give them their food in due season.
You open wide your hand,
grant the desires of all who live.

You are just in all your ways
and loving in all your deeds.
You are close to all who call you,
who call on you from their hearts.

You grant the desires of those who fear you,
you hear their cry and you save them.
LORD, you protect all who love you;
but the wicked you will utterly destroy.

Let me speak your praise, O LORD,
Let all peoples bless your holy name
for ever, for ages unending.

Thanksgiving

My heart is ready, O God;
I will sing your praise.
Your steadfast love is higher than the heavens,
and your faithfulness reaches to the clouds.
(free prayers of thanksgiving)
Be exalted, O God, above the heavens,
and let your glory shine over all the earth.
Amen.

Song

Praise to the Lord, the Almighty (H37)
Many and great, O God (H35)
We gather together (H17)

Call to discipleship

Jesus said, Let anyone with ears to hear listen.
You shall love the Lord your God
with all your heart, and with all your soul,
and with all your strength,

and with all your mind;
and your neighbor as yourself.
Do this, and you will live.
Lord Jesus, you have the words of eternal life.

Luke 18.1-8

Then Jesus told them a parable about their
need to pray always and not to lose heart. He
said, "In a certain city there was a judge who
neither feared God nor had respect for people.
In that city there was a widow who kept
coming to him and saying, 'Grant me justice
against my opponent.' For a while he refused;
but later he said to himself, 'Though I have
no fear of God and no respect for anyone, yet
because this widow keeps bothering me, I will
grant her justice, so that she may not wear me
out by continually coming.'" And the Lord
said, "Listen to what the unjust judge says.
And will not God grant justice to his chosen
ones who cry to him day and night? Will he
delay long in helping them? I tell you, he will
quickly grant justice to them. And yet, when
the Son of Man comes, will he find faith on
earth?"

1 Thessalonians 5.14-21

And we [Paul, Silvanus, and Timothy] urge
you, beloved, to admonish the idlers, encourage the faint hearted, help the weak, be

patient with all of them. See that none of you repays evil for evil, but always seek to do good to one another and to all. Rejoice always, pray without ceasing, give thanks in all circumstances; for this is the will of God in Christ Jesus for you. Do not quench the Spirit. Do not despise the words of prophets, but test everything; hold fast to what is good.

Silent or spoken reflection on the readings

Song
All praise to our redeeming Lord (H21)
O Master, let me walk with thee (H357)
Lord Jesus, you shall be my song (SJ14)

Zechariah's song

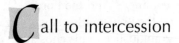# *C*all to intercession

Rejoice in the Lord always.
The Lord is near.
Do not worry about anything,
but in everything with thanksgiving
let your requests be made known to God.

God, our help and hope, we bring our prayers to you as acts of love for you and for our neighbors.
In your mercy, Lord, hear our prayer.

You have been our help from one generation to the next. We pray for ourselves and those dear to us.
(open prayers)
We will bless you as long as we live, O God; ***hear our prayer.***

You are present in strangers. We pray for our community and for our neighbors.
(open prayers)
We will bless you as long as we live, O God; ***hear our prayer.***

You look to find faith on earth. We pray for the church in all places, that we may bear witness to your reign of justice, peace, and joy.
(open prayers)
We will bless you as long as we live, O God; ***hear our prayer.***

Your right hand is filled with justice. We pray for the world, for all who are ensnared in greed, violence, and oppression.
(open prayers)
We will bless you as long as we live, O God; ***hear our prayer.***

We offer you other concerns we carry in our hearts.
(open prayers)
We will bless you as long as we live, O God; ***hear our prayer.***

Gracious God,
you sow your storied word in us
with compassion.
As this day breaks upon us,
may we remember your mercy
and extend it to others
as we live for the sake of your reign.
In hope we pray:

Our Father ...

Benediction

May the Lord bless us and keep us.
May the face of God shine on us
and be gracious to us.
May God's presence embrace us
and give us peace. Amen.

Our ancestors have told us

Opening sentence

I will open my mouth in a parable
and reveal hidden lessons of the past.
The things we have heard and understood,
the things our ancestors have told us,
these we will not hide from their children.

*C*all to praise

O God, your word is a lamp to my feet
and a light to my path.
The light and peace of Jesus Christ be with us.

Glory ...

Psalm 48.10-15 [9-14]

God, we ponder your love
within your temple.
Your praise, O God, like your name
reaches the ends of the earth.

With justice your right hand is filled.
Mount Zion rejoices;
the people of Judah rejoice
at the sight of your judgments.

Walk through Zion, walk all around it;
count the number of its towers.
Review all its ramparts,
examine its castles,

that you may tell the next generation
that such is our God,
our God for ever and ever
will always lead us.

Thanksgiving

It is good to give thanks to the Lord,
to sing praises to your name, O Most High.
(free prayers of thanksgiving)
We declare your steadfast love in the morning,
and your faithfulness by night. Amen.

Song

Je louerai l'Eternel (Praise, I will praise you,
   Lord) (H76)
O come, loud anthems let us sing (H68)
Open now thy gates of beauty (H19)

Confession

Have mercy on me, O God,
according to your steadfast love;
according to your abundant mercy
blot out my transgressions.
(silence)
Create in me a clean heart, O God,
and put a new and right spirit within me.

Restore to me the joy of your salvation
and sustain in me a willing spirit. Amen.

Call to discipleship

Jesus said, I am the bread of life.
Whoever comes to me will never be hungry,
and whoever believes in me
will never be thirsty.
Lord Jesus, you have the words of eternal life.

Matthew 25.(31-33), 34-40

"Then the king will say to those at his right
hand, 'Come, you that are blessed by my
Father, inherit the kingdom prepared for you
from the foundation of the world; for I was
hungry and you gave me food, I was thirsty
and you gave me something to drink, I was a
stranger and you welcomed me, I was naked
and you gave me clothing, I was sick and you
took care of me, I was in prison and you visited
me. Then the righteous will answer him, 'Lord,
when was it that we saw you hungry and gave
you food, or thirsty and gave you something
to drink? And when was it that we saw you
a stranger and welcomed you, or naked and
gave you clothing? And when was it that we
saw you sick or in prison and visited you? And
the king will answer them, 'Truly I tell you, just

as you did it to one of the least of these who
are members of my family, you did it to me.'"

Isaiah 58.9-11

If you remove the yoke from among you,
the pointing of the finger, the speaking of evil,
if you offer your food to the hungry
and satisfy the needs of the afflicted,
then your light shall rise in the darkness
and your gloom be like the noonday.
The LORD will guide you continually,
and satisfy your needs in parched places,
and make your bones strong;
and you shall be like a watered garden,
like a spring of water, whose waters never fail.

Silent or spoken reflection on the readings

Song

Lord, whose love in humble service (H369)
Brothers and sisters of mine (H142)
Jesus Christ is waiting (SJ30)

Mary's *or* Simeon's song

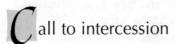

Call to intercession

Ask, and it will be given you;
search, and you will find;
knock, and the door will be opened for you.

The heavenly Father will give the Holy Spirit to those who ask.

God, our help and hope, we bring our prayers to you with confidence, in the name of our Lord Jesus.
In your mercy, Lord, hear our prayer.

You have been our help from one generation to the next. We pray for ourselves and those dear to us.
(open prayers)
We will bless you as long as we live, O God;
hear our prayer.

You are present in strangers. We pray for our community and for our neighbors.
(open prayers)
We will bless you as long as we live, O God;
hear our prayer.

You look to find faith on earth. We pray for the church in all places, that we may bear witness to your reign of justice, peace, and joy.
(open prayers)
We will bless you as long as we live, O God;
hear our prayer.

Your right hand is filled with justice. We pray for the world, for all who are ensnared in greed, violence, and oppression.
(open prayers)

We will bless you as long as we live, O God;
hear our prayer.

We offer you other concerns we carry in our
hearts.
(open prayers)
We will bless you as long as we live, O God;
hear our prayer.

Generous God,
you draw us into surprising stories.
Use them to disrupt our complacency
and remove our fear,
that we may follow you
into the joy of your kingdom.
In the name of the one
who taught us not to lose heart, we pray:

Our Father …

Benediction
*May God, who supplies seed to the sower
and bread for food,
supply and multiply our seed for sowing
and increase the harvest
of our righteousness. Amen.*

Setting a witness

WEEK 3 PARABLES

Opening sentence

I will open my mouth in a parable
and reveal hidden lessons of the past.
We will tell them to the next generation:
the glories and might of the Lord
and the marvelous deeds God has done,
setting a witness in Jacob,
and establishing the law in Israel.

*C*all to praise

Lord, open our lips
and our mouths will proclaim your praise.
You are good to those who wait for you,
to all who seek you.

Glory ...

Psalm 119.57-64

My part, I have resolved, O LORD,
is to obey your word.
With all my heart I implore your favor;
show the mercy of your promise.
I have pondered over my ways
and returned to your will.

I made haste and did not delay
to obey your commands.
Though the nets of the wicked ensnared me
I remembered your law.
At midnight I will rise and thank you
for your just decrees.
I am a friend of all who revere you,
who obey your precepts.
LORD, *your love fills the earth.*
Teach me your statutes.

Thanksgiving

My heart is ready, O God;
I will sing your praise.
Your steadfast love is higher than the heavens,
and your faithfulness reaches to the clouds.
(free prayers of thanksgiving)
Be exalted, O God, above the heavens,
and let your glory shine over all the earth.
Amen.

Song

Our Father God, thy name we praise (H32)
Blessed Jesus, at your word (H13)
Rejoice, rejoice in God (H313)

Call to discipleship

Jesus said, Let anyone with ears to hear listen.
You shall love the Lord your God
with all your heart, and with all your soul,
and with all your strength,
and with all your mind;
and your neighbor as yourself.
Do this, and you will live.
Lord Jesus, you have the words of eternal life.

Matthew 21.28-31

"What do you think? A man had two sons; he
went to the first and said, 'Son, go and work
in the vineyard today.' He answered, 'I will
not'; but later he changed his mind and went.
The father went to the second and said the
same; and he answered, 'I go, sir'; but he did
not go. Which of the two did the will of his
father?"

James 1.22-27

But be doers of the word, and not merely
hearers who deceive themselves. For if any
are hearers of the word and not doers, they
are like those who look at themselves in a mirror; for they look at themselves and, on going
away, immediately forget what they were like.
But those who look into the perfect law, the
law of liberty, and persevere, being not hear-

ers who forget but doers who act—they will be blessed in their doing.

If any think they are religious, and do not bridle their tongues but deceive their hearts, their religion is worthless. Religion that is pure and undefiled before God, the Father, is this: to care for orphans and widows in their distress, and to keep oneself unstained by the world.

Silent or spoken reflection on the readings

Song
Holy Spirit, gracious Guest (H542)
God of the Bible (SJ27)
How clear is our vocation, Lord (H541)

Zechariah's song

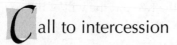

*C*all to intercession

Rejoice in the Lord always.
The Lord is near.
Do not worry about anything,
but in everything with thanksgiving
let your requests be made known to God.

God of persistent patience, we bring our prayers to you as acts of love for you and for our neighbors.
In your mercy, Lord, hear our prayer.

Your word is trustworthy. We pray for ourselves and those dear to us.
(open prayers)
Turn to us and be gracious to us, Lord;
hear our prayer.

You show the mercy of your promise. We pray for our community and for our neighbors.
(open prayers)
Turn to us and be gracious to us, Lord;
hear our prayer.

You are not slow about your promise, and are patient with us. We pray for the church in all places, that we may daily follow in the footsteps of Christ.
(open prayers)
Turn to us and be gracious to us, Lord;
hear our prayer.

Your just love fills the earth. We pray for the world, for those in positions of power and authority.
(open prayers)
Turn to us and be gracious to us, Lord;
hear our prayer.

We offer you other concerns we carry in our hearts.
(open prayers)
Turn to us and be gracious to us, Lord;
hear our prayer.

Gracious God,
you sow your storied word in us
with compassion.
As this day breaks upon us,
may we remember your mercy
and extend it to others
as we live for the sake of your reign.
In hope we pray:

Our Father ...

Benediction
May we lead lives worthy of the Lord,
fully pleasing to him,
as we bear fruit in every good work
and as we grow in the knowledge of God.
Amen.

Setting a witness

Opening sentence

I will open my mouth in a parable
and reveal hidden lessons of the past.
We will tell them to the next generation:
the glories and might of the Lord
and the marvelous deeds God has done,
setting a witness in Jacob,
and establishing the law in Israel.

*C*all to praise

O God, your word is a lamp to my feet
and a light to my path.
The light and peace of Jesus Christ be with us.

Glory ...

Psalm 119.129-136

Your will is wonderful indeed;
therefore I obey it.
The unfolding of your word gives light
and teaches the simple.
I open my mouth and I sigh
as I yearn for your commands.
Turn and show me your mercy;
show justice to your friends.

Let my steps be guided by your promise;
let no evil rule me.
Redeem me from those who oppress me
and I will keep your precepts.
Let your face shine on your servant
and teach me your decrees.
Tears stream from my eyes
because your law is disobeyed.

Thanksgiving

It is good to give thanks to the Lord,
to sing praises to your name, O Most High.
(free prayers of thanksgiving)
We declare your steadfast love in the morning,
and your faithfulness by night. Amen.

Song

I long for your commandments (H543)
Lord, I have made thy word (H317)
This is a story full of love (H315)

Confession

Have mercy on me, O God,
according to your steadfast love;
according to your abundant mercy
blot out my transgressions.
(silence)
Create in me a clean heart, O God,
and put a new and right spirit within me.
Restore to me the joy of your salvation
and sustain in me a willing spirit. Amen.

Call to discipleship

Jesus said, I am the bread of life.
Whoever comes to me will never be hungry,
and whoever believes in me
will never be thirsty.
Lord Jesus, you have the words of eternal life.

Luke 12.35-40

"Be dressed for action and have your lamps
lit; be like those who are waiting for their
master to return from the wedding banquet,
so that they may open the door for him as
soon as he comes and knocks. Blessed are
those slaves whom the master finds alert
when he comes; truly I tell you, he will fasten
his belt and have them sit down to eat, and he
will come and serve them. If he comes during
the middle of the night, or near dawn, and
finds them so, blessed are those slaves.

"But know this: if the owner of the house had
known at what hour the thief was coming, he
would not have let his house be broken into.
You also must be ready, for the Son of Man is
coming at an unexpected hour."

2 Peter 3.8-9

But do not ignore this one fact, beloved, that
with the Lord one day is like a thousand

years, and a thousand years are like one day.
The Lord is not slow about his promise, as
some think of slowness, but is patient with
you, not wanting any to perish, but all to
come to repentance.

Silent or spoken reflection on the readings

Song
Jesus came—the heavens adoring (H297)
Keep your lamps trimmed (SS118)
Oh, how shall I receive thee (H182)

Mary's *or* Simeon's song

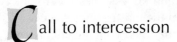 all to intercession

Ask, and it will be given you;
search, and you will find;
knock, and the door will be opened for you.
*The heavenly Father will give the Holy Spirit
to those who ask.*

God of persistent patience, we bring our
prayers to you with confidence, in the name
of our Lord Jesus.
In your mercy, Lord, hear our prayer.

Your word is trustworthy. We pray for ourselves and those dear to us.
(open prayers)

Turn to us and be gracious to us, Lord;
hear our prayer.

You show the mercy of your promise. We pray
for our community and for our neighbors.
(open prayers)
Turn to us and be gracious to us, Lord;
hear our prayer.

You are not slow about your promise, and are
patient with us. We pray for the church in all
places, that we may daily follow in the footsteps of Christ.
(open prayers)
Turn to us and be gracious to us, Lord;
hear our prayer.

Your just love fills the earth. We pray for the
world, for those in positions of power and
authority.
(open prayers)
Turn to us and be gracious to us, Lord;
hear our prayer.

We offer you other concerns we carry in our
hearts.
(open prayers)
Turn to us and be gracious to us, Lord;
hear our prayer.

Generous God,
you draw us into surprising stories.

Use them to disrupt our complacency
and remove our fear,
that we may follow you
into the joy of your kingdom.
In the name of the one
who taught us not to lose heart, we pray:

Our Father ...

Benediction
*May we be filled
with the knowledge of God's will
in all spiritual wisdom and understanding.
Amen.*

That the next generation might know

WEEK 3 PARABLES

Opening sentence

Give heed, my people, to my teaching;
I will open my mouth in a parable.
God gave a command to our ancestors
to make it known to their children
that the next generation might know it,
the children yet to be born.

Call to praise

Lord, open our lips
and our mouths will proclaim your praise.
You are good to those who wait for you,
to all who seek you.

Glory …

Psalm 25.1-7

To you, O LORD, I lift up my soul.
My God, I trust you,
let me not be disappointed;
do not let my enemies triumph.

Those who hope in you
   shall not be disappointed,
but only those who wantonly break faith.

LORD, make me know your ways.
LORD, teach me your paths.
Make me walk in your truth, and teach me,
for you are God my savior.

In you I hope all the day long
because of your goodness, O LORD.
Remember your mercy, LORD,
and the love you have shown from of old.
Do not remember the sins of my youth.
In your love remember me.

Thanksgiving

My heart is ready, O God;
I will sing your praise.
Your steadfast love is higher than the heavens,
and your faithfulness reaches to the clouds.
(free prayers of thanksgiving)
Be exalted, O God, above the heavens,
and let your glory shine over all the earth.
Amen.

Song

O Christe Domine Jesu (H113, with Psalm 25
   verses)
My Shepherd will supply my need (H589)
God is our refuge and strength (SJ26)

Call to discipleship

Jesus said, Let anyone with ears to hear listen.
You shall love the Lord your God
with all your heart, and with all your soul,
and with all your strength,
and with all your mind;
and your neighbor as yourself.
Do this, and you will live.
Lord Jesus, you have the words of eternal life.

Mark 13.32-37

"But about that day or hour no one knows,
neither the angels in heaven, nor the Son, but
only the Father. Beware, keep alert; for you do
not know when the time will come. It is like a
man going on a journey, when he leaves home
and puts his slaves in charge, each with his
work, and commands the doorkeeper to be on
the watch. Therefore, keep awake—for you
do not know when the master of the house
will come, in the evening, or at midnight, or at
cockcrow, or at dawn, or else he may find you
asleep when he comes suddenly. And what I
say to you I say to all: Keep awake."

1 Peter 4.7-11

The end of all things is near; therefore be seri-
ous and discipline yourselves for the sake of
your prayers. Above all, maintain constant

love for one another, for love covers a multitude of sins. Be hospitable to one another without complaining. Like good stewards of the manifold grace of God, serve one another with whatever gift each of you has received. Whoever speaks must do so as one speaking the very words of God; whoever serves must do so with the strength that God supplies, so that God may be glorified in all things through Jesus Christ. To him belong the glory and the power forever and ever. Amen.

Silent or spoken reflection on the readings

Song

Christ is coming! Let creation (H295)
Come, thou long-expected Jesus (H178)
Awake, awake, fling off the night (H448)

Zechariah's song

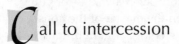 all to intercession

Rejoice in the Lord always.
The Lord is near.
Do not worry about anything,
but in everything with thanksgiving
let your requests be made known to God.

God of manifold grace, we bring our prayers to you as acts of love for you and for our neighbors.
In your mercy, Lord, hear our prayer.

You are always there to lead us. We pray for ourselves and those dear to us.
(open prayers)
We put our hope in you, Lord;
hear our prayer.

You supply strength for service. We pray for our community and for our neighbors.
(open prayers)
We put our hope in you, Lord;
hear our prayer.

You call your people to speak the very words of God. We pray for the church in all places, that we may speak boldly for Christ.
(open prayers)
We put our hope in you, Lord;
hear our prayer.

You will make justice break forth like the light. We pray for the world, for all who do justice and love mercy.
(open prayers)
We put our hope in you, Lord;
hear our prayer.

We offer you other concerns we carry in our
hearts.
(open prayers)
We put our hope in you, Lord;
hear our prayer.

Gracious God,
you sow your storied word in us
with compassion.
As this day breaks upon us,
may we remember your mercy
and extend it to others
as we live for the sake of your reign.
In hope we pray:

Our Father …

Benediction
And after we have suffered for a little while,
the God of all grace,
who has called us to eternal glory in Christ,
will restore, support, strengthen,
and establish us. Amen.

That the next generation might know

WEEK 3 PARABLES

Opening sentence

Give heed, my people, to my teaching;
I will open my mouth in a parable.
God gave a command to our ancestors
to make it known to their children
that the next generation might know it,
the children yet to be born.

Call to praise

O God, your word is a lamp to my feet
and a light to my path.
The light and peace of Jesus Christ be with us.

Glory ...

Psalm 71.15-19

My lips will tell of your justice
and day by day of your help
(though I can never tell it all).

LORD, I will declare your mighty deeds,
proclaiming your justice, yours alone.
O God, you have taught me from my youth
and I proclaim your wonder still.

Now that I am old and gray-headed,
do not forsake me, God.
Let me tell of your power to all ages,
praise your strength and justice to the skies,
tell of you who have worked such wonders.
O God, who is like you?

Thanksgiving

It is good to give thanks to the Lord,
to sing praises to your name, O Most High.
(free prayers of thanksgiving)
We declare your steadfast love in the morning,
and your faithfulness by night. Amen.

Song

Sing praise to God who reigns (H59)
Now thank we all our God (H85, 86)
I'll praise my Maker (H166)

Confession

Have mercy on me, O God,
according to your steadfast love;
according to your abundant mercy
blot out my transgressions.
(silence)
Create in me a clean heart, O God,
and put a new and right spirit within me.
Restore to me the joy of your salvation
and sustain in me a willing spirit. Amen.

*C*all to discipleship

Jesus said, I am the bread of life.
Whoever comes to me will never be hungry,
and whoever believes in me
will never be thirsty.
Lord Jesus, you have the words of eternal life.

Matthew 13.44-46

"The kingdom of heaven is like treasure hidden in a field, which someone found and hid; then in his joy he goes and sells all that he has and buys that field.

"Again, the kingdom of heaven is like a merchant in search of fine pearls; on finding one pearl of great value, he went and sold all that he had and bought it."

Romans 12.1-2

I appeal to you therefore, brothers and sisters, by the mercies of God, to present your bodies as a living sacrifice, holy and acceptable to God, which is your spiritual worship. Do not be conformed to this world, but be transformed by the renewing of your minds, so that you may discern what is the will of God—what is good and acceptable and perfect.

Silent or spoken reflection on the readings

Song
   Gracious Spirit, dwell with me (H507)
   Eternal Light, shine in my heart (H518)
   Take my life (H389)

Mary's *or* Simeon's song

*C*all to intercession

Ask, and it will be given you;
search, and you will find;
knock, and the door will be opened for you.
*The heavenly Father will give the Holy Spirit
to those who ask.*

God of manifold grace, we bring our prayers
to you with confidence, in the name of our
Lord Jesus.
In your mercy, Lord, hear our prayer.

You are always there to lead us. We pray for
ourselves and those dear to us.
(open prayers)
We put our hope in you, Lord;
hear our prayer.

You supply strength for service. We pray for
our community and for our neighbors.
(open prayers)

We put our hope in you, Lord;
hear our prayer.

You call your people to speak the very words
of God. We pray for the church in all places,
that we may speak boldly for Christ.
(open prayers)
We put our hope in you, Lord;
hear our prayer.

You will make justice break forth like the
light. We pray for the world, for all who do
justice and love mercy.
(open prayers)
We put our hope in you, Lord;
hear our prayer.

We offer you other concerns we carry in our
hearts.
(open prayers)
We put our hope in you, Lord;
hear our prayer.

Generous God,
you draw us into surprising stories.
Use them to disrupt our complacency
and remove our fear,
that we may follow you
into the joy of your kingdom.
In the name of the one
who taught us not to lose heart, we pray:

Our Father ...

Benediction
*By the tender mercy of our God,
the dawn from on high will break upon us,
to give light to those who sit in darkness
and in the shadow of death,
to guide our feet into the way of peace. Amen.*

They too should hope in God

Opening sentence

Give heed, my people, to my teaching;
I will open my mouth in a parable.
The next generation too should arise
and tell their children
that they too should set their hope in God.

Call to praise

Lord, open our lips
and our mouths will proclaim your praise.
You are good to those who wait for you,
to all who seek you.

Glory ...

Psalm 71.5-8

It is you, O Lord, who are my hope,
my trust, O Lord, since my youth.
On you I have leaned from my birth;
from my mother's womb
you have been my help.
My hope has always been in you.

My fate has filled many with awe
but you are my strong refuge.

My lips are filled with your praise,
with your glory all the day long.

Thanksgiving

My heart is ready, O God;
I will sing your praise.
Your steadfast love is higher than the heavens,
and your faithfulness reaches to the clouds.
(free prayers of thanksgiving)
Be exalted, O God, above the heavens,
and let your glory shine over all the earth.
Amen.

Song

God created heaven and earth (H160)
O God, your constant care (H481)
Lord, with devotion we pray (H79)

Call to discipleship

Jesus said, Let anyone with ears to hear listen.
You shall love the Lord your God
with all your heart, and with all your soul,
and with all your strength,
and with all your mind;
and your neighbor as yourself.
Do this, and you will live.
Lord Jesus, you have the words of eternal life.

Matthew 20.(1-7), 8-16

"When evening came, the owner of the vineyard said to his manager, 'Call the laborers
and give them their pay, beginning with the
last and then going to the first.' When those
hired about five o'clock came, each of them
received the usual daily wage. Now when the
first came, they thought they would receive
more; but each of them also received the
usual daily wage. And when they received it,
they grumbled against the landowner, saying, 'These last worked only one hour, and
you have made them equal to us who have
borne the burden of the day and the scorching heat.' But he replied to one of them,
'Friend, I am doing you no wrong; did you
not agree with me for the usual daily wage?
Take what belongs to you and go; I choose to
give to this last the same as I give to you. Am
I not allowed to do what I choose with what
belongs to me? Or are you envious because I
am generous?' So the last will be first, and the
first will be last."

Ezekiel 18.29-32

Yet the house of Israel says, "The way of the
Lord is unfair." O house of Israel, are my
ways unfair? Is it not your ways that are
unfair?

Therefore I will judge you, O house of Israel, all of you according to your ways, says the Lord GOD. Repent and turn from all your transgressions; otherwise iniquity will be your ruin. Cast away from you all the transgressions that you have committed against me, and get yourselves a new heart and a new spirit! Why will you die, O house of Israel? For I have no pleasure in the death of anyone, says the Lord GOD. Turn, then, and live.

Silent or spoken reflection on the readings

Song
God, whose giving (H383)
There's a wideness in God's mercy (H145)
Come, thou fount (H521)

Zechariah's song

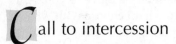

Call to intercession

Rejoice in the Lord always.
The Lord is near.
Do not worry about anything,
but in everything with thanksgiving
let your requests be made known to God.

God of hope, we bring our prayers to you as acts of love for you and for our neighbors.
In your mercy, Lord, hear our prayer.

You protect those who trust in you. We pray for ourselves and those dear to us.
(open prayers)
You are gracious and just, O Lord;
hear our prayer.

You invite all people, so that your house may be filled. We pray for our community and for our neighbors.
(open prayers)
You are gracious and just, O Lord;
hear our prayer.

You are holy, and your decrees abide forever. We pray for the church in all places, that we may be faithful in solidarity across generations and geography.
(open prayers)
You are gracious and just, O Lord;
hear our prayer.

You will destroy the shroud cast over all peoples. We pray for the world, for our enemies and for those who are in conflict.
(open prayers)
You are gracious and just, O Lord;
hear our prayer.

We offer you other concerns we carry in our hearts.
(open prayers)
You are gracious and just, O Lord;
hear our prayer.

Gracious God,
you sow your storied word in us
with compassion.
As this day breaks upon us,
may we remember your mercy
and extend it to others
as we live for the sake of your reign.
In hope we pray:

Our Father ...

Benediction
May the God of peace sanctify us entirely;
and may our spirit and soul and body
be kept sound and blameless
at the coming of our Lord Jesus Christ.
The one who calls us is faithful
and will do this. Amen.

They too should hope in God

WEEK 3 PARABLES

Opening sentence

Give heed, my people, to my teaching;
I will open my mouth in a parable.
The next generation too should arise
and tell their children
that they too should set their hope in God.

*C*all to praise

O God, your word is a lamp to my feet
and a light to my path.
The light and peace of Jesus Christ be with us.

Glory ...

Psalm 116.2-9

The LORD was attentive to me
in the day when I called.

They surrounded me, the snares of death,
with the anguish of the tomb;
they caught me, sorrow and distress.
I called on the LORD's name.

O LORD, my God, deliver me!

How gracious is the LORD, and just;
our God has compassion.
The LORD protects the simple hearts;
I was helpless so God saved me.

Turn back, my soul, to your rest
for the LORD has been good,
and has kept my soul from death,
(my eyes from tears,)
my feet from stumbling.

I will walk in the presence of the LORD
in the land of the living.

Thanksgiving

It is good to give thanks to the Lord,
to sing praises to your name, O Most High.
(free prayers of thanksgiving)
We declare your steadfast love in the morning,
and your faithfulness by night. Amen.

Song

Praise, praise, praise the Lord! (SJ11)
We give thanks unto you (H161)
Great is thy faithfulness (H327)

Confession

Have mercy on me, O God,
according to your steadfast love;
according to your abundant mercy
blot out my transgressions.
(silence)

Create in me a clean heart, O God,
and put a new and right spirit within me.
Restore to me the joy of your salvation
and sustain in me a willing spirit. Amen.

Call to discipleship

Jesus said, I am the bread of life.
Whoever comes to me will never be hungry,
and whoever believes in me
will never be thirsty.
Lord Jesus, you have the words of eternal life.

Luke 14.16-24

Then Jesus said to him, "Someone gave a
great dinner and invited many. At the time
for the dinner he sent his slave to say to those
who had been invited, 'Come, for everything
is ready now.' But they all alike began to make
excuses. The first said to him, 'I have bought
a piece of land, and I must go out and see
it; please accept my regrets.' Another said, 'I
have bought five yoke of oxen, and I am going
to try them out; please accept my regrets.'
Another said, 'I have just been married, and
therefore I cannot come.' So the slave returned
and reported this to his master. Then the
owner of the house became angry and said to
his slave, 'Go out at once into the streets and

lanes of the town and bring in the poor, the crippled, the blind, and the lame.' And the slave said, 'Sir, what you ordered has been done, and there is still room.' Then the master said to the slave, 'Go out into the roads and lanes, and compel people to come in, so that my house may be filled. For I tell you, none of those who were invited will taste my dinner.'"

Isaiah 25.6-9

On this mountain the LORD of hosts will make
    for all peoples
a feast of rich food, a feast of well-aged wines,
of rich food filled with marrow, of well-aged
    wines strained clear.
And he will destroy on this mountain
the shroud that is cast over all peoples,
the sheet that is spread over all nations;
he will swallow up death forever.
Then the Lord GOD will wipe away the tears
    from all faces,
and the disgrace of his people he will take
    away from all the earth,
for the LORD has spoken.

It will be said on that day,
Lo, this is our God; we have waited for him,
    so that he might save us.
This is the LORD for whom we have waited;
let us be glad and rejoice in his salvation.

Silent or spoken reflection on the readings

Song
God loves all his many people (H397)
This is the feast of victory (H476)
You've got a place (SJ4)

Mary's *or* Simeon's song

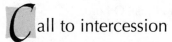# Call to intercession

Ask, and it will be given you;
search, and you will find;
knock, and the door will be opened for you.
***The heavenly Father will give the Holy Spirit
to those who ask.***

God of hope, we bring our prayers to you
with confidence, in the name of our Lord
Jesus.
In your mercy, Lord, hear our prayer.

You protect those who trust in you. We pray
for ourselves and those dear to us.
(open prayers)
You are gracious and just, O Lord;
hear our prayer.

You invite all people, so that your house may
be filled. We pray for our community and for
our neighbors.

(open prayers)
You are gracious and just, O Lord;
hear our prayer.

You are holy, and your decrees abide forever.
We pray for the church in all places, that we
may be faithful in solidarity across generations and geography.
(open prayers)
You are gracious and just, O Lord;
hear our prayer.

You will destroy the shroud cast over all peoples. We pray for the world, for our enemies
and for those who are in conflict.
(open prayers)
You are gracious and just, O Lord;
hear our prayer.

We offer you other concerns we carry in our
hearts.
(open prayers)
You are gracious and just, O Lord;
hear our prayer.

Generous God,
you draw us into surprising stories.
Use them to disrupt our complacency
and remove our fear,
that we may follow you
into the joy of your kingdom.

In the name of the one
who taught us not to lose heart, we pray:

Our Father ...

Benediction

*May the God of steadfastness
and encouragement
grant us to live in harmony with one another,
in accordance with Christ Jesus,
so that together we may with one voice
glorify the God and Father
of our Lord Jesus Christ. Amen.*

Signs and Wonders

The Spirit of the Lord is upon me

WEEK 4 SIGNS AND WONDERS

Opening sentence

Jesus unrolled the scroll
and found the place where it was written:
"The Spirit of the Lord is upon me."

*C*all to praise

Lord, open our lips
and our mouths will proclaim your praise.
You are good to those who wait for you,
to all who seek you.

Glory ...

Psalm 20.2-9 [1-8]

May the LORD answer in time of trial;
may the name of Jacob's God protect you.

May God send you help from the shrine
and give you support from Zion;
remember all your offerings
and receive your sacrifice with favor.

May God give you your heart's desire
and fulfill every one of your plans.
May we ring out our joy at your victory
and rejoice in the name of our God.
May the LORD grant all your prayers.

I am sure now that the LORD
will give victory to his anointed,
will reply from his holy heaven
with a mighty victorious hand.

Some trust in chariots or horses,
but we in the name of the LORD.
They will collapse and fall,
but we shall hold and stand firm.

Thanksgiving

My heart is ready, O God;
I will sing your praise.
Your steadfast love is higher than the heavens,
and your faithfulness reaches to the clouds.
(free prayers of thanksgiving)
Be exalted, O God, above the heavens,
and let your glory shine over all the earth. Amen.

Song

Christ is the world's true light (H334)
The Lord is King (H69)
Blessing and honor and glory (H108)

Call to discipleship

Jesus said, Let anyone with ears to hear listen.
You shall love the Lord your God
with all your heart, and with all your soul,
and with all your strength,

and with all your mind;
and your neighbor as yourself.
Do this, and you will live.
Lord Jesus, you have the words of eternal life.

Matthew 12.15-20

Many crowds followed [Jesus], and he cured
all of them, and he ordered them not to make
him known. This was to fulfill what had been
spoken through the prophet Isaiah:

> "Here is my servant, whom I have chosen,
> my beloved, with whom my soul is well
>   pleased.
> I will put my Spirit upon him,
> and he will proclaim justice to the
>   Gentiles.
> He will not wrangle or cry aloud,
> nor will anyone hear his voice in the
>   streets.
> He will not break a bruised reed
> or quench a smoldering wick
> until he brings justice to victory."

Acts 4.24-31

When [the believers heard that Peter and John
had been released], they raised their voices
together to God and said, "Sovereign Lord,
who made the heaven and the earth, the sea,
and everything in them, it is you who said by

the Holy Spirit through our ancestor David,
your servant:

'Why did the Gentiles rage,
and the peoples imagine vain things?
The kings of the earth took their stand,
and the rulers have gathered together
against the Lord and against his Messiah.'

For in this city, in fact, both Herod and
Pontius Pilate, with the Gentiles and the peoples of Israel, gathered together against your
holy servant Jesus, whom you anointed, to do
whatever your hand and your plan had pre-
destined to take place. And now, Lord, look
at their threats, and grant to your servants to
speak your word with all boldness, while you
stretch out your hand to heal, and signs and
wonders are performed through the name
of your holy servant Jesus." When they had
prayed, the place in which they were gathered
together was shaken; and they were all filled
with the Holy Spirit and spoke the word of
God with boldness.

Silent or spoken reflection on the readings

Song
Spirit of God, unleashed on earth (H364)
O Jesus Christ, may grateful hymns (H404)
O Spirit of the living God (H361)

Zechariah's song

*C*all to intercession

Rejoice in the Lord always.
The Lord is near.
Do not worry about anything,
but in everything with thanksgiving
let your requests be made known to God.

God who works wonders, we bring our
prayers to you as acts of love for you and for
our neighbors.
In your mercy, Lord, hear our prayer.

You are our helper, whatever our need. We
pray for ourselves and those dear to us.
(open prayers)
We put our trust in you, Lord;
hear our prayer.

Your presence dispels fear. We pray for our
community and for our neighbors.
(open prayers)
We put our trust in you, Lord;
hear our prayer.

You are the strength and song of your people.
We pray for the church in all places, that we
may be one.
(open prayers)
We put our trust in you, Lord;
hear our prayer.

Your Spirit breathes forgiveness and peace.
We pray for the world, that your reign may
come and your will be done on earth.
(open prayers)
We put our trust in you, Lord;
hear our prayer.

We offer you other concerns we carry in our
hearts.
(open prayers)
We put our trust in you, Lord;
hear our prayer.

God whose grace touches us
in our unworthiness,
you come near and speak the healing word.
Reveal to us this day a sign of your glory,
that we might listen to your voice
and walk in your ways.
Through Jesus our Lord,
who taught us to pray:

Our Father ...

Benediction
Now may the God of peace,
who brought back from the dead
our Lord Jesus,
make us complete in everything good
so that we may do God's will,
through Jesus Christ,
to whom be the glory forever and ever. Amen.

The Spirit of the Lord is upon me

Opening sentence

Jesus unrolled the scroll
and found the place where it was written:
"The Spirit of the Lord is upon me."

*C*all to praise

O God, your word is a lamp to my feet
and a light to my path.
The light and peace of Jesus Christ be with us.

Glory …

Psalm 118.13-17

I was thrust down, thrust down and falling,
but the LORD was my helper.
The LORD is my strength and my song;
and has been my savior.
There are shouts of joy and victory
in the tents of the just.

The LORD's right hand has triumphed;
God's right hand raised me.
The LORD's right hand has triumphed;
I shall not die, I shall live
and recount God's deeds.

Thanksgiving

It is good to give thanks to the Lord,
to sing praises to your name, O Most High.
(free prayers of thanksgiving)
We declare your steadfast love in the morning,
and your faithfulness by night. Amen.

Song

Gloria (H204)
I will sing the Lord's high triumph (H261)
My soul is filled with joy (SJ13)

Confession

Have mercy on me, O God,
according to your steadfast love;
according to your abundant mercy
blot out my transgressions.
(silence)
Create in me a clean heart, O God,
and put a new and right spirit within me.
Restore to me the joy of your salvation
and sustain in me a willing spirit. Amen.

Call to discipleship

Jesus said, I am the bread of life.
Whoever comes to me will never be hungry,
and whoever believes in me
will never be thirsty.
Lord Jesus, you have the words of eternal life.

John 20.19-23

When it was evening on that day, the first day of the week, and the doors of the house where the disciples had met were locked for fear of the Jews, Jesus came and stood among them and said, "Peace be with you." After he said this, he showed them his hands and his side. Then the disciples rejoiced when they saw the Lord. Jesus said to them again, "Peace be with you. As the Father has sent me, so I send you." When he had said this, he breathed on them and said to them, "Receive the Holy Spirit. If you forgive the sins of any, they are forgiven them; if you retain the sins of any, they are retained."

2 Corinthians 3.17-18

Now the Lord is the Spirit, and where the Spirit of the Lord is, there is freedom. And all of us, with unveiled faces, seeing the glory of the Lord as though reflected in a mirror, are being transformed into the same image from one degree of glory to another; for this comes from the Lord, the Spirit.

Silent or spoken reflection on the readings

Song

Filled with the Spirit's power (H289)
Lord divine, all loves excelling (H592)
Spirit, working in creation (SJ10)

Mary's *or* Simeon's song

*C*all to intercession

Ask, and it will be given you;
search, and you will find;
knock, and the door will be opened for you.
The heavenly Father will give the Holy Spirit
to those who ask.

God who works wonders, we bring our
prayers to you with confidence, in the name
of our Lord Jesus.
In your mercy, Lord, hear our prayer.

You are our helper, whatever our need. We
pray for ourselves and those dear to us.
(open prayers)
We put our trust in you, Lord;
hear our prayer.

Your presence dispels fear. We pray for our
community and for our neighbors.
(open prayers)
We put our trust in you, Lord;
hear our prayer.

You are the strength and song of your people.
We pray for the church in all places, that we
may be one.
(open prayers)

We put our trust in you, Lord;
hear our prayer.

Your Spirit breathes forgiveness and peace.
We pray for the world, that your reign may
come and your will be done on earth.
(open prayers)
We put our trust in you, Lord;
hear our prayer.

We offer you other concerns we carry in our
hearts.
(open prayers)
We put our trust in you, Lord;
hear our prayer.

Wondrous God,
who raised Jesus from death to life,
you heal the wounds that our swords inflict
and deliver us from fear to faith.
Grant us trust in your saving power,
that we might know your restoring touch
this night
and rise tomorrow to sing your praise.
Through Jesus the Savior,
in whose name we pray:

Our Father ...

Benediction
*Now may the God of peace,
who brought back from the dead*

our Lord Jesus,
make us complete in everything good
so that we may do God's will,
through Jesus Christ,
to whom be the glory forever and ever. Amen.

He has anointed me

WEEK 4 SIGNS AND WONDERS

Opening sentence

Jesus unrolled the scroll
and found the place where it was written:
*"The Spirit of the Lord is upon me
because he has anointed me."*

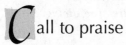all to praise

Lord, open our lips
and our mouths will proclaim your praise.
You are good to those who wait for you,
to all who seek you.

Glory ...

Psalm 105.1-5, 40-43

Give thanks, and acclaim God's name,
make known God's deeds among the peoples.

*O sing to the Lord, sing praise;
tell all his wonderful works!*
Be proud of God's holy name,
let the hearts that seek the LORD rejoice.

*Consider the LORD, who is strong;
constantly seek his face.*

Remember the wonders of the LORD,
the miracles and judgments pronounced.

When they asked for food God sent quails;
and filled them with bread from heaven.
The Lord pierced the rock; water gushed;
it flowed in the desert like a river.

For God remembered the holy promise,
which was given to Abraham, his servant.
God brought out the people with joy,
the chosen ones with shouts of rejoicing.

Thanksgiving

My heart is ready, O God;
I will sing your praise.
Your steadfast love is higher than the heavens,
and your faithfulness reaches to the clouds.
(free prayers of thanksgiving)
Be exalted, O God, above the heavens,
and let your glory shine over all the earth.
Amen.

Song

Jubilate Deo omnis terra (H103)
Great is the Lord (H87)
Who is so great a God (H62)

Call to discipleship

Jesus said, Let anyone with ears to hear listen.
You shall love the Lord your God
with all your heart, and with all your soul,
and with all your strength,
and with all your mind;
and your neighbor as yourself.
Do this, and you will live.
Lord Jesus, you have the words of eternal life.

John 2.1-11

There was a wedding in Cana of Galilee, and the mother of Jesus was there. Jesus and his disciples had also been invited to the wedding. When the wine gave out, the mother of Jesus said to him, "They have no wine." And Jesus said to her, "Woman, what concern is that to you and to me? My hour has not yet come." His mother said to the servants, "Do whatever he tells you." Now standing there were six stone water jars for the Jewish rites of purification, each holding twenty or thirty gallons. Jesus said to them, "Fill the jars with water." And they filled them up to the brim. He said to them, "Now draw some out, and take it to the chief steward." So they took it. When the steward tasted the water that had become wine, and did not know where it came from (though the servants who had drawn the water knew), the steward called the bridegroom and said to him, "Everyone serves the good wine first, and then the inferior wine after the guests have become drunk. But you have kept the good wine until now." Jesus did this, the first of his signs, in Cana of Galilee, and revealed his glory; and his disciples believed in him.

2 Corinthians 4.6

For it is the God who said, "Let light shine out of darkness," who has shone in our hearts to give the light of the knowledge of the glory of God in the face of Jesus Christ.

Silent or spoken reflection on the readings

Song

Lord, you sometimes speak (H594)
I sing with exultation (H438)
Christ, whose glory fills the skies (H216)

Zechariah's song

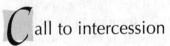# Call to intercession

Rejoice in the Lord always.
The Lord is near.

Do not worry about anything,
but in everything with thanksgiving
let your requests be made known to God.

God who gives life to our souls, we bring our prayers to you as acts of love for you and for our neighbors.
In your mercy, Lord, hear our prayer.

You offer us the water of life. We pray for ourselves and those dear to us.
(open prayers)
You give life to our souls, Lord;
hear our prayer.

You surprise us with generosity. We pray for our community and for our neighbors.
(open prayers)
You give life to our souls, Lord;
hear our prayer.

You are the joy of your people. We pray for the church in all places, that we may know the freedom of life in the Spirit.
(open prayers)
You give life to our souls, Lord;
hear our prayer.

Your eyes keep watch over the nations. We pray for the world and for all who care for creation.
(open prayers)

You give life to our souls, Lord;
hear our prayer.

We offer you other concerns we carry in our
hearts.
(open prayers)
You give life to our souls, Lord;
hear our prayer.

God whose grace touches us
in our unworthiness,
you come near and speak the healing word.
Reveal to us this day a sign of your glory,
that we might listen to your voice
and walk in your ways.
Through Jesus our Lord,
who taught us to pray:

Our Father ...

Benediction
*Now to God,
who by the power at work within us
is able to accomplish abundantly far more
than all we can ask or imagine,
be glory in the church and in Christ Jesus
to all generations, forever and ever. Amen.*

He has anointed me

Opening sentence

Jesus unrolled the scroll
and found the place where it was written:
*"The Spirit of the Lord is upon me
because he has anointed me."*

*C*all to praise

O God, your word is a lamp to my feet
and a light to my path.
The light and peace of Jesus Christ be with us.

Glory ...

Psalm 66.1-9

Cry out with joy to God all the earth,
O sing to the glory of his name
rendering glorious praise.
Say to God: "How tremendous your deeds!

Because of the greatness of your strength
your enemies cringe before you.
*Before you all the earth shall bow,
shall sing to you, sing to your name!"*

Come and see the works of God,
tremendous deeds for the people.

God turned the sea into dry land,
they passed through the river dry-shod.

Let your joy then be in the Lord,
who rules forever in power,
whose eyes keep watch over nations;
let rebels not lift themselves up.

O peoples, bless our God;
let the voice of God's praise resound,
of the God who gave life to our souls
and kept our feet from stumbling.

Thanksgiving

It is good to give thanks to the Lord,
to sing praises to your name, O Most High.
(free prayers of thanksgiving)
We declare your steadfast love in the morning,
and your faithfulness by night. Amen.

Song

Let the whole creation cry (H51)
From all that dwell below the skies (H49)
To God be the glory (H102)

Confession

Have mercy on me, O God,
according to your steadfast love;
according to your abundant mercy
blot out my transgressions.
(silence)

Create in me a clean heart, O God,
and put a new and right spirit within me.
Restore to me the joy of your salvation
and sustain in me a willing spirit. Amen.

*C*all to discipleship

Jesus said, I am the bread of life.
Whoever comes to me will never be hungry,
and whoever believes in me
will never be thirsty.
Lord Jesus, you have the words of eternal life.

Mark 6.(34-38), 39-44

[Jesus] ordered [the disciples] to get all the
people to sit down in groups on the green
grass. So they sat down in groups of hundreds
and of fifties. Taking the five loaves and the
two fish, he looked up to heaven, and blessed
and broke the loaves, and gave them to his
disciples to set before the people; and he
divided the two fish among them all. And all
ate and were filled; and they took up twelve
baskets full of broken pieces and of the fish.
Those who had eaten the loaves numbered
five thousand men.

2 Kings 4.42-44

A man came ... bringing food from the first
fruits to the man of God: twenty loaves of bar-

ley and fresh ears of grain in his sack. Elisha said, "Give it to the people and let them eat." But his servant said, "How can I set this before a hundred people?" So he repeated, "Give it to the people and let them eat, for thus says the LORD, 'They shall eat and have some left.'" He set it before them, they ate, and had some left, according to the word of the LORD.

Silent or spoken reflection on the readings

Song

Break thou the bread of life (H360)
I hunger and I thirst (H474)
Shepherd of souls, refresh (H456, vv. 1-3)

Mary's *or* Simeon's song

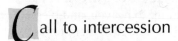

*C*all to intercession

Ask, and it will be given you;
search, and you will find;
knock, and the door will be opened for you.
***The heavenly Father will give the Holy Spirit
to those who ask.***

God who gives life to our souls, we bring our prayers to you with confidence, in the name of our Lord Jesus.
In your mercy, Lord, hear our prayer.

You offer us the water of life. We pray for ourselves and those dear to us.
(open prayers)
You give life to our souls, Lord;
hear our prayer.

You surprise us with generosity. We pray for our community and for our neighbors.
(open prayers)
You give life to our souls, Lord;
hear our prayer.

You are the joy of your people. We pray for the church in all places, that we may know the freedom of life in the Spirit.
(open prayers)
You give life to our souls, Lord;
hear our prayer.

Your eyes keep watch over the nations. We pray for the world and for all who care for creation.
(open prayers)
You give life to our souls, Lord;
hear our prayer.

We offer you other concerns we carry in our hearts.
(open prayers)
You give life to our souls, Lord;
hear our prayer.

Wondrous God,
who raised Jesus from death to life,
you heal the wounds that our swords inflict
and deliver us from fear to faith.
Grant us trust in your saving power,
that we might know your restoring touch this night
and rise tomorrow to sing your praise.
Through Jesus the Savior,
in whose name we pray:

Our Father ...

Benediction
Peace be to the whole community,
and love with faith,
from God the Father
and the Lord Jesus Christ. Amen.

Good news to the poor

Opening sentence

Jesus unrolled the scroll
and found the place where it was written:
"The Spirit of the Lord is upon me
because he has anointed me
to bring good news to the poor."

*C*all to praise

Lord, open our lips
and our mouths will proclaim your praise.
You are good to those who wait for you,
to all who seek you.

Glory ...

Psalm 72.12-14

For he shall save the poor when they cry
and the needy who are helpless.
He will have pity on the weak
and save the lives of the poor.

From oppression he will rescue their lives,
to him their blood is dear.

Thanksgiving

My heart is ready, O God;
I will sing your praise.
Your steadfast love is higher than the heavens,
and your faithfulness reaches to the clouds.
(free prayers of thanksgiving)
Be exalted, O God, above the heavens,
and let your glory shine over all the earth.
Amen.

Song

Hail to the Lord's anointed (H185)
Creating God, your fingers trace (H168)
Praise with joy the world's Creator (SJ16)

*C*all to discipleship

Jesus said, Let anyone with ears to hear listen.
You shall love the Lord your God
with all your heart, and with all your soul,
and with all your strength,
and with all your mind;
and your neighbor as yourself.
Do this, and you will live.
Lord Jesus, you have the words of eternal life.

Mark 1.40-45

A leper came to [Jesus] begging him, and
kneeling he said to him, "If you choose, you
can make me clean." Moved with pity, Jesus

stretched out his hand and touched him, and said to him, "I do choose. Be made clean!" Immediately the leprosy left him, and he was made clean. After sternly warning him he sent him away at once, saying to him, "See that you say nothing to anyone; but go, show yourself to the priest, and offer for your cleansing what Moses commanded, as a testimony to them." But he went out and began to proclaim it freely, and to spread the word, so that Jesus could no longer go into a town openly, but stayed out in the country; and people came to him from every quarter.

Acts 4.5-14

The next day [the] rulers, elders, and scribes assembled in Jerusalem, with Annas the high priest, Caiaphas, John, and Alexander, and all who were of the high-priestly family. When they had made the prisoners stand in their midst, they inquired, "By what power or by what name did you do this?" Then Peter, filled with the Holy Spirit, said to them, "Rulers of the people and elders, if we are questioned today because of a good deed done to someone who was sick and are asked how this man has been healed, let it be known to all of you, and to all the people of Israel, that this man is standing before you in good health by the name of Jesus Christ of

Nazareth, whom you crucified, whom God raised from the dead. This Jesus is

'the stone that was rejected by you, the builders; it has become the cornerstone.'

There is salvation in no one else, for there is no other name under heaven given among mortals by which we must be saved."

Now when they saw the boldness of Peter and John and realized that they were uneducated and ordinary men, they were amazed and recognized them as companions of Jesus. When they saw the man who had been cured standing beside them, they had nothing to say in opposition.

Silent or spoken reflection on the readings

Song
   O Christ, the healer (H379)
   Heal us, Immanuel, here we are (H375)
   O God, thou faithful God (H376)

Zechariah's song

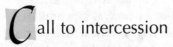 all to intercession

Rejoice in the Lord always.
The Lord is near.

Do not worry about anything,
but in everything with thanksgiving
let your requests be made known to God.

God of healing power, we bring our prayers
to you as acts of love for you and for our
neighbors.
In your mercy, Lord, hear our prayer.

You are lamp and light for our life. We pray
for ourselves and those dear to us.
(open prayers)
We entrust ourselves to you, Lord;
hear our prayer.

You hear the prayer of those who are in trouble. We pray for our community and for our
neighbors.
(open prayers)
We entrust ourselves to you, Lord;
hear our prayer.

You redeem us from sin. We pray for the
church in all places, that we may reflect your
faithful love.
(open prayers)
We entrust ourselves to you, Lord;
hear our prayer.

You break the power of the wicked. We pray
for the world, for those who are in need.
(open prayers)

We entrust ourselves to you, Lord;
hear our prayer.

We offer you other concerns we carry in our hearts.
(open prayers)
We entrust ourselves to you, Lord;
hear our prayer.

God whose grace touches us
in our unworthiness,
you come near and speak the healing word.
Reveal to us this day a sign of your glory,
that we might listen to your voice
and walk in your ways.
Through Jesus our Lord,
who taught us to pray:

Our Father ...

Benediction
*May the Lord direct our hearts
to the love of God
and to the steadfastness of Christ. Amen.*

Good news to the poor

Opening sentence

Jesus unrolled the scroll
and found the place where it was written:
"The Spirit of the Lord is upon me
because he has anointed me
to bring good news to the poor."

Call to praise

O God, your word is a lamp to my feet
and a light to my path.
The light and peace of Jesus Christ be with us.

Glory ...

Psalm 10.12-18

Arise then, LORD, lift up your hand!
O God, do not forget the poor!
Why should the wicked spurn the LORD
and think in their hearts:
   "God will not punish"?

But you have seen the trouble and sorrow,
you note it, you take it in hand.
The helpless entrust themselves to you,
for you are the helper of the orphan.

Break the power of the wicked and the sinner!
Punish their wickedness till nothing remains!
The LORD is king for ever and ever.
The heathen shall perish
from the land of the Lord.

LORD, you hear the prayer of the poor;
you strengthen their hearts; you turn your ear
to protect the rights of the orphan
and oppressed
so that those from the earth may strike terror
no more.

Thanksgiving

It is good to give thanks to the Lord,
to sing praises to your name, O Most High.
(free prayers of thanksgiving)
We declare your steadfast love in the morning,
and your faithfulness by night. Amen.

Song

Now thank we all our God (H85)
A mighty fortress is our God (H165)
Oh, for a thousand tongues to sing (H110)

Confession

Have mercy on me, O God,
according to your steadfast love;
according to your abundant mercy
blot out my transgressions.
(silence)

Create in me a clean heart, O God,
and put a new and right spirit within me.
Restore to me the joy of your salvation
and sustain in me a willing spirit. Amen.

Call to discipleship

Jesus said, I am the bread of life.
Whoever comes to me will never be hungry,
and whoever believes in me
will never be thirsty.
Lord Jesus, you have the words of eternal life.

Luke 8.43-48

Now there was a woman who had been suffering from hemorrhages for twelve years;
and though she had spent all she had on
physicians, no one could cure her. She came
up behind Jesus and touched the fringe of
his clothes, and immediately her hemorrhage
stopped. Then Jesus asked, "Who touched
me?" When all denied it, Peter said, "Master,
the crowds surround you and press in on
you." But Jesus said, "Someone touched me;
for I noticed that power had gone out from
me." When the woman saw that she could not
remain hidden, she came trembling; and falling down before him, she declared in the presence of all the people why she had touched

him, and how she had been immediately healed. He said to her, "Daughter, your faith has made you well; go in peace."

Ephesians 2.8-10

For by grace you have been saved through faith, and this is not your own doing; it is the gift of God—not the result of works, so that no one may boast. For we are what he has made us, created in Christ Jesus for good works, which God prepared beforehand to be our way of life.

Silent or spoken reflection on the readings

Song

Just as I am, without one plea (H516)
At evening, when the sun had set (H628)
By Peter's house (H378)

Mary's *or* Simeon's song

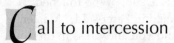all to intercession

Ask, and it will be given you;
search, and you will find;
knock, and the door will be opened for you.
The heavenly Father will give the Holy Spirit to those who ask.

God of healing power, we bring our prayers to you with confidence, in the name of our Lord Jesus.
In your mercy, Lord, hear our prayer.

You are lamp and light for our life. We pray for ourselves and those dear to us.
(open prayers)
We entrust ourselves to you, Lord;
hear our prayer.

You hear the prayer of those who are in trouble. We pray for our community and for our neighbors.
(open prayers)
We entrust ourselves to you, Lord;
hear our prayer.

You redeem us from sin. We pray for the church in all places, that we may reflect your faithful love.
(open prayers)
We entrust ourselves to you, Lord;
hear our prayer.

You break the power of the wicked. We pray for the world, for those who are in need.
(open prayers)
We entrust ourselves to you, Lord;
hear our prayer.

We offer you other concerns we carry in our hearts.
(open prayers)
We entrust ourselves to you, Lord;
hear our prayer.

Wondrous God,
who raised Jesus from death to life,
you heal the wounds that our swords inflict
and deliver us from fear to faith.
Grant us trust in your saving power,
that we might know your restoring touch
this night
and rise tomorrow to sing your praise.
Through Jesus the Savior,
in whose name we pray:

Our Father ...

Benediction

*Now may the Lord of peace
give us peace at all times in all ways.
The Lord be with us. Amen.*

Release to the captives

WEEK 4 SIGNS AND WONDERS

Opening sentences
Jesus unrolled the scroll
and found the place where it was written:
"The Spirit of the Lord is upon me
because he has anointed me
to bring good news to the poor.
He has sent me
to proclaim release to the captives."

Call to praise

Lord, open our lips
and our mouths will proclaim your praise.
You are good to those who wait for you,
to all who seek you.

Glory ...

Psalm 107.10-16
Some lay in darkness and in gloom,
prisoners in misery and chains,
having defied the words of God
and spurned the counsels of the Most High.
God crushed their spirit with toil;
they stumbled; there was no one to help.

*Then they cried to the L*ORD *in their need*
and he rescued them from their distress,
led them forth from darkness and gloom
and broke their chains to pieces.

*Let them confess the love of the L*ORD,
the wonders God does for the people,
bursting the gates of bronze,
shattering the iron bars.

Thanksgiving

My heart is ready, O God;
I will sing your praise.
Your steadfast love is higher than the heavens,
and your faithfulness reaches to the clouds.
(*free prayers of thanksgiving*)
Be exalted, O God, above the heavens,
and let your glory shine over all the earth.
Amen.

Song

Hark! the glad sound (H184)
Bless'd be the God of Israel (H174)
Christ, whose glory fills the skies (H216)

Call to discipleship

Jesus said, Let anyone with ears to hear listen.
You shall love the Lord your God
with all your heart, and with all your soul,

and with all your strength,
and with all your mind;
and your neighbor as yourself.
Do this, and you will live.
Lord Jesus, you have the words of eternal life.

Mark 9.14-29

When [Jesus, Peter, John, and James returned
to the rest of] the disciples, they saw a great
crowd around them, and some scribes arguing
with them. When the whole crowd saw him,
they were immediately overcome with awe,
and they ran forward to greet him. He asked
them, "What are you arguing about with
them?" Someone from the crowd answered
him, "Teacher, I brought you my son; he
has a spirit that makes him unable to speak;
and whenever it seizes him, it dashes him
down; and he foams and grinds his teeth and
becomes rigid; and I asked your disciples
to cast it out, but they could not do so." He
answered them, "You faithless generation,
how much longer must I be among you? How
much longer must I put up with you? Bring
him to me." And they brought the boy to
him. When the spirit saw him, immediately it
convulsed the boy, and he fell on the ground
and rolled about, foaming at the mouth. Jesus
asked the father, "How long has this been
happening to him?" And he said, "From child-

hood. It has often cast him into the fire and into the water, to destroy him; but if you are able to do anything, have pity on us and help us." Jesus said to him, "If you are able!—All things can be done for the one who believes." Immediately the father of the child cried out, "I believe; help my unbelief!" When Jesus saw that a crowd came running together, he rebuked the unclean spirit, saying to it, "You spirit that keeps this boy from speaking and hearing, I command you, come out of him, and never enter him again!" After crying out and convulsing him terribly, it came out, and the boy was like a corpse, so that most of them said, "He is dead." But Jesus took him by the hand and lifted him up, and he was able to stand. When he had entered the house, his disciples asked him privately, "Why could we not cast it out?" He said to them, "This kind can come out only through prayer."

2 Corinthians 12.7-10

Therefore, to keep me from being too elated, a thorn was given me in the flesh, a messenger of Satan to torment me, to keep me from being too elated. Three times I appealed to the Lord about this, that it would leave me, but he said to me, "My grace is sufficient for you, for power is made perfect in weakness." So, I will boast all the more gladly of my weaknesses,

so that the power of Christ may dwell in me.
Therefore I am content with weaknesses,
insults, hardships, persecutions, and calamities for the sake of Christ; for whenever I am
weak, then I am strong.

Silent or spoken reflection on the readings

Song
Cast thy burden upon the Lord (H586)
Silence! frenzied, unclean spirit (H630)
How firm a foundation (H567)

Zechariah's song

Call to intercession

Rejoice in the Lord always.
The Lord is near.
Do not worry about anything,
but in everything with thanksgiving
let your requests be made known to God.

God of redemption, we bring our prayers
to you as acts of love for you and for our
neighbors.
In your mercy, Lord, hear our prayer.

Your grace is sufficient for us. We pray for
ourselves and those dear to us.
(open prayers)

You bring release to the captives, Lord;
hear our prayer.

You heal the brokenhearted and bind up all
their wounds. We pray for our community
and for our neighbors.
(open prayers)
You bring release to the captives, Lord;
hear our prayer.

You show your healing power through your
people. We pray for the church in all places,
that we may bear witness to your reign of justice, peace, and joy.
(open prayers)
You bring release to the captives, Lord;
hear our prayer.

Your wisdom is beyond measure. We pray for
the world, for all who are ensnared in greed,
violence, and oppression.
(open prayers)
You bring release to the captives, Lord;
hear our prayer.

We offer you other concerns we carry in our
hearts.
(open prayers)
You bring release to the captives, Lord;
hear our prayer.

God whose grace touches us
in our unworthiness,
you come near and speak the healing word.
Reveal to us this day a sign of your glory,
that we might listen to your voice
and walk in your ways.
Through Jesus our Lord,
who taught us to pray:

Our Father ...

Benediction
May God our Savior,
through Jesus Christ our Lord,
keep us from falling,
and make us stand without blemish
in the presence of his glory with rejoicing.
Amen.

Release to the captives

Opening sentences
Jesus unrolled the scroll
and found the place where it was written:
"The Spirit of the Lord is upon me
because he has anointed me
to bring good news to the poor.
He has sent me
to proclaim release to the captives."

Call to praise

O God, your word is a lamp to my feet
and a light to my path.
The light and peace of Jesus Christ be with us.

Glory ...

Psalm 147.1-7
Alleluia!

Sing praise to the LORD who is good;
sing to our God who is loving:
to God our praise is due.

The LORD builds up Jerusalem
and brings back Israel's exiles,

God heals the broken-hearted,
and binds up all their wounds.
God fixes the number of the stars;
and calls each one by its name.

Our Lord is great and almighty;
God's wisdom can never be measured.
The LORD raises the lowly;
and humbles the wicked to the dust.
O sing to the LORD, giving thanks;
sing psalms to our God with the harp.

Thanksgiving

It is good to give thanks to the Lord,
to sing praises to your name, O Most High.
(free prayers of thanksgiving)
We declare your steadfast love in the morning,
and your faithfulness by night. Amen.

Song

Alleluia (SJ41)
Praise God from whom (H118, 119)
Amen (H643)

Confession

Have mercy on me, O God,
according to your steadfast love;
according to your abundant mercy
blot out my transgressions.
(silence)

Create in me a clean heart, O God,
and put a new and right spirit within me.
*Restore to me the joy of your salvation
and sustain in me a willing spirit. Amen.*

Call to discipleship

Jesus said, I am the bread of life.
Whoever comes to me will never be hungry,
and whoever believes in me
will never be thirsty.
Lord Jesus, you have the words of eternal life.

John 5.1-9

There was a festival of the Jews, and Jesus
went up to Jerusalem.

Now in Jerusalem by the Sheep Gate there is a
pool, called in Hebrew Beth-zatha, which has
five porticoes. In these lay many invalids—
blind, lame, and paralyzed. One man was
there who had been ill for thirty-eight years.
When Jesus saw him lying there and knew
that he had been there a long time, he said
to him, "Do you want to be made well?" The
sick man answered him, "Sir, I have no one to
put me into the pool when the water is stirred
up; and while I am making my way, someone
else steps down ahead of me." Jesus said to
him, "Stand up, take your mat and walk." At

once the man was made well, and he took up his mat and began to walk.

Now that day was a sabbath.

Acts 5.12-16

Now many signs and wonders were done among the people through the apostles. And they were all together in Solomon's Portico. None of the rest dared to join them, but the people held them in high esteem. Yet more than ever believers were added to the Lord, great numbers of both men and women, so that they even carried out the sick into the streets, and laid them on cots and mats, in order that Peter's shadow might fall on some of them as he came by. A great number of people would also gather from the towns around Jerusalem, bringing the sick and those tormented by unclean spirits, and they were all cured.

Silent or spoken reflection on the readings

Song

My faith has found a resting place (SJ43)
The Lord lift you up (SJ73)
Healing balm, forgiving Lord (SJ55)

Mary's *or* Simeon's song

*C*all to intercession

Ask, and it will be given you;
search, and you will find;
knock, and the door will be opened for you.
*The heavenly Father will give the Holy Spirit
to those who ask.*

God of redemption, we bring our prayers to
you with confidence, in the name of our Lord
Jesus.
In your mercy, Lord, hear our prayer.

Your grace is sufficient for us. We pray for
ourselves and those dear to us.
(open prayers)
You bring release to the captives, Lord;
hear our prayer.

You heal the brokenhearted and bind up all
their wounds. We pray for our community
and for our neighbors.
(open prayers)
You bring release to the captives, Lord;
hear our prayer.

You show your healing power through your
people. We pray for the church in all places,
that we may bear witness to your reign of justice, peace, and joy.
(open prayers)

You bring release to the captives, Lord;
hear our prayer.

Your wisdom is beyond measure. We pray for
the world, for all who are ensnared in greed,
violence, and oppression.
(open prayers)
You bring release to the captives, Lord;
hear our prayer.

We offer you other concerns we carry in our
hearts.
(open prayers)
You bring release to the captives, Lord;
hear our prayer.

Wondrous God,
who raised Jesus from death to life,
you heal the wounds that our swords inflict
and deliver us from fear to faith.
Grant us trust in your saving power,
that we might know your restoring touch
this night
and rise tomorrow to sing your praise.
Through Jesus the Savior,
in whose name we pray:

Our Father ...

Benediction
May God our Savior,
through Jesus Christ our Lord,

keep us from falling,
and make us stand without blemish
in the presence of his glory with rejoicing.
Amen.

Recovery of sight

Opening sentences

Jesus unrolled the scroll
and found the place where it was written:
"The Spirit of the Lord is upon me
because he has anointed me
to bring good news to the poor.
He has sent me
to proclaim release to the captives
and recovery of sight to the blind."

Call to praise

Lord, open our lips
and our mouths will proclaim your praise.
You are good to those who wait for you,
to all who seek you.

Glory ...

Psalm 111.1-4

Alleluia!

I will thank the LORD with all my heart
in the meeting of the just and their assembly.
Great are the works of the LORD,
to be pondered by all who love them.

Majestic and glorious God's work,
whose justice stands firm for ever.
God makes us remember these wonders.
The LORD is compassion and love.

Thanksgiving

My heart is ready, O God;
I will sing your praise.
Your steadfast love is higher than the heavens,
and your faithfulness reaches to the clouds.
(free prayers of thanksgiving)
Be exalted, O God, above the heavens,
and let your glory shine over all the earth.
Amen.

Song

With all my heart I offer (H432)
Halle, halle, hallelujah! (SJ17)
I will stand (SS113)

Call to discipleship

Jesus said, Let anyone with ears to hear listen.
You shall love the Lord your God
with all your heart, and with all your soul,
and with all your strength,
and with all your mind;
and your neighbor as yourself.
Do this, and you will live.
Lord Jesus, you have the words of eternal life.

Mark 10.46-52

As [Jesus] and his disciples and a large crowd were leaving Jericho, Bartimaeus son of Timaeus, a blind beggar, was sitting by the roadside. When he heard that it was Jesus of Nazareth, he began to shout out and say, "Jesus, Son of David, have mercy on me!" Many sternly ordered him to be quiet, but he cried out even more loudly, "Son of David, have mercy on me!" Jesus stood still and said, "Call him here." And they called the blind man, saying to him, "Take heart; get up, he is calling you." So throwing off his cloak, he sprang up and came to Jesus. Then Jesus said to him, "What do you want me to do for you?" The blind man said to him, "My teacher, let me see again." Jesus said to him, "Go; your faith has made you well." Immediately he regained his sight and followed him on the way.

Acts 26.12-18

"I [Paul] was traveling to Damascus with the authority and commission of the chief priests, when at midday along the road, your Excellency, I saw a light from heaven, brighter than the sun, shining around me and my companions. When we had all fallen to the ground, I heard a voice saying to me in the Hebrew language, 'Saul, Saul, why are you persecuting me? It hurts you to kick against the goads.' I asked, 'Who are you, Lord?' The Lord answered, 'I am Jesus whom you are persecuting. But get up and stand on your feet; for I have appeared to you for this purpose, to appoint you to serve and testify to the things in which you have seen me and to those in which I will appear to you. I will rescue you from your people and from the Gentiles—to whom I am sending you to open their eyes so that they may turn from darkness to light and from the power of Satan to God, so that they may receive forgiveness of sins and a place among those who are sanctified by faith in me.'

Silent or spoken reflection on the readings

Song
    'Tis not with eyes of flesh we see (H571)
    We walk by faith (H570)
    Come and be light for our eyes (SJ5)

Zechariah's song

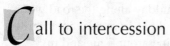

*C*all to intercession

Rejoice in the Lord always.
The Lord is near.

Do not worry about anything,
but in everything with thanksgiving
let your requests be made known to God.

Faithful God, we bring our prayers to you as
acts of love for you and for our neighbors.
In your mercy, Lord, hear our prayer.

You give us breath every day. We pray for
ourselves and those dear to us.
(open prayers)
You keep faith forever, Lord;
hear our prayer.

You protect the stranger and uphold the
widow and the orphan. We pray for our community and for our neighbors.
(open prayers)
You keep faith forever, Lord;
hear our prayer.

Your help is the hope of your people. We pray
for the church in all places, that we may daily
follow in the footsteps of Christ.
(open prayers)
You keep faith forever, Lord;
hear our prayer.

Your justice stands firm forever. We pray for
the world, for those in positions of power and
authority.
(open prayers)

You keep faith forever, Lord;
hear our prayer.

We offer you other concerns we carry in our
hearts.
(open prayers)
You keep faith forever, Lord;
hear our prayer.

God whose grace touches us
in our unworthiness,
you come near and speak the healing word.
Reveal to us this day a sign of your glory,
that we might listen to your voice
and walk in your ways.
Through Jesus our Lord,
who taught us to pray:

Our Father ...

Benediction
The Lord will keep us from all evil;
the Lord will keep our life.
The Lord will keep our going out
and our coming in
from this time on and forevermore. Amen.

Recovery of sight

WEEK 4 SIGNS AND WONDERS

Opening sentences

Jesus unrolled the scroll
and found the place where it was written:
"The Spirit of the Lord is upon me
because he has anointed me
to bring good news to the poor.
He has sent me
to proclaim release to the captives
and recovery of sight to the blind."

Call to praise

O God, your word is a lamp to my feet
and a light to my path.
The light and peace of Jesus Christ be with us.

Glory ...

Psalm 146.1-9

Alleluia!

My soul, give praise to the LORD;
I will praise the LORD all my days,
make music to my God while I live.

Put no trust in the powerful,
mere mortals in whom there is no help.

Take their breath, they return to clay
and their plans that day come to nothing.

They are happy who are helped by Jacob's God,
whose hope is in the LORD their God,
who alone made heaven and earth,
the seas and all they contain.

It is the LORD who keeps faith for ever,
who is just to those who are oppressed.
It is God who gives bread to the hungry,
the LORD, who sets prisoners free,

the LORD who gives sight to the blind,
who raises up those who are bowed down,
the LORD, who protects the stranger
and upholds the widow and orphan.

Thanksgiving

It is good to give thanks to the Lord,
to sing praises to your name, O Most High.
(free prayers of thanksgiving)
We declare your steadfast love in the morning,
and your faithfulness by night. Amen.

Song

I'll praise my Maker (H166)
Alleluia (H101)
Asithi: Amen (Sing amen) (H64)

Confession

Have mercy on me, O God,
according to your steadfast love;
according to your abundant mercy
blot out my transgressions.
(silence)
Create in me a clean heart, O God,
and put a new and right spirit within me.
Restore to me the joy of your salvation
and sustain in me a willing spirit. Amen.

C all to discipleship

Jesus said, I am the bread of life.
Whoever comes to me will never be hungry,
and whoever believes in me
will never be thirsty.
Lord Jesus, you have the words of eternal life.

Mark 8.22-26

[Jesus and the disciples] came to Bethsaida.
Some people brought a blind man to him and
begged him to touch him. He took the blind
man by the hand and led him out of the village; and when he had put saliva on his eyes
and laid his hands on him, he asked him,
"Can you see anything?" And the man looked
up and said, "I can see people, but they look
like trees, walking." Then Jesus laid his hands

on his eyes again; and he looked intently and his sight was restored, and he saw everything clearly. Then he sent him away to his home, saying, "Do not even go into the village."

Acts 22.6-15

"While I [Paul] was on my way and approaching Damascus, about noon a great light from heaven suddenly shone about me. I fell to the ground and heard a voice saying to me, 'Saul, Saul, why are you persecuting me?' I answered, 'Who are you, Lord?' Then he said to me, 'I am Jesus of Nazareth whom you are persecuting.' Now those who were with me saw the light but did not hear the voice of the one who was speaking to me. I asked, 'What am I to do, Lord?' The Lord said to me, 'Get up and go to Damascus; there you will be told everything that has been assigned to you to do.' Since I could not see because of the brightness of that light, those who were with me took my hand and led me to Damascus.

"A certain Ananias, who was a devout man according to the law and well spoken of by all the Jews living there, came to me; and standing beside me, he said, 'Brother Saul, regain your sight!' In that very hour I regained my sight and saw him. Then he said, 'The God of our ancestors has chosen you to know his

will, to see the Righteous One and to hear his
own voice; for you will be his witness to all
the world of what you have seen and heard.'"

Silent or spoken reflection on the readings

Song

O praise the gracious power (H111, vv. 1, 2, 4, 7)
Who has known the mind of Jesus? (SJ58)
Here I am, Lord (H395, refrain only)

Mary's *or* Simeon's song

Call to intercession

Ask, and it will be given you;
search, and you will find;
knock, and the door will be opened for you.
***The heavenly Father will give the Holy Spirit
to those who ask.***

Faithful God, we bring our prayers to you
with confidence, in the name of our Lord
Jesus.
In your mercy, Lord, hear our prayer.

You give us breath every day. We pray for
ourselves and those dear to us.
(open prayers)
You keep faith forever, Lord;
hear our prayer.

You protect the stranger and uphold the widow and the orphan. We pray for our community and for our neighbors.
(open prayers)
You keep faith forever, Lord;
hear our prayer.

Your help is the hope of your people. We pray for the church in all places, that we may daily follow in the footsteps of Christ.
(open prayers)
You keep faith forever, Lord;
hear our prayer.

Your justice stands firm forever. We pray for the world, for those in positions of power and authority.
(open prayers)
You keep faith forever, Lord;
hear our prayer.

We offer you other concerns we carry in our hearts.
(open prayers)
You keep faith forever, Lord;
hear our prayer.

Wondrous God,
who raised Jesus from death to life,
you heal the wounds that our swords inflict
and deliver us from fear to faith.
Grant us trust in your saving power,

that we might know your restoring touch
this night
and rise tomorrow to sing your praise.
Through Jesus the Savior,
in whose name we pray:

Our Father ...

Benediction
The Lord will keep us from all evil;
the Lord will keep our life.
The Lord will keep our going out
and our coming in
from this time on and forevermore. Amen.

The oppressed go free

Opening sentences

Jesus unrolled the scroll
and found the place where it was written:
"The Spirit of the Lord is upon me
because he has anointed me
to bring good news to the poor.
He has sent me
to proclaim release to the captives
and recovery of sight to the blind,
to let the oppressed go free."

*C*all to praise

Lord, open our lips
and our mouths will proclaim your praise.
You are good to those who wait for you,
to all who seek you.

Glory ...

Psalm 61.2-6 [1-5]

O God, hear my cry!
Listen to my prayer!
From the end of the earth I call;
my heart is faint.

On a rock too high for me to reach
set me on high,
O you who have been my refuge,
my tower against the foe.

Let me dwell in your tent for ever
and hide in the shelter of your wings.
For you, O God, hear my prayer,
grant me the heritage of those who fear you.

Thanksgiving

My heart is ready, O God;
I will sing your praise.
Your steadfast love is higher than the heavens,
and your faithfulness reaches to the clouds.
(free prayers of thanksgiving)
Be exalted, O God, above the heavens,
and let your glory shine over all the earth.
Amen.

Song

As morning breaks (SJ114)
For mornings bright (SJ113)
Fire of God, undying Flame (H129/SS103)

Call to discipleship

Jesus said, Let anyone with ears to hear listen.
You shall love the Lord your God
with all your heart, and with all your soul,

and with all your strength,
and with all your mind;
and your neighbor as yourself.
Do this, and you will live.
Lord Jesus, you have the words of eternal life.

Mark 3.1-6

Again [Jesus] entered the synagogue, and a
man was there who had a withered hand.
They watched him to see whether he would
cure him on the sabbath, so that they might
accuse him. And he said to the man who had
the withered hand, "Come forward." Then he
said to them, "Is it lawful to do good or to do
harm on the sabbath, to save life or to kill?"
But they were silent. He looked around at
them with anger; he was grieved at their hard-
ness of heart and said to the man, "Stretch out
your hand." He stretched it out, and his hand
was restored. The Pharisees went out and
immediately conspired with the Herodians
against him, how to destroy him.

Isaiah 58.6-9

Is not this the fast that I choose:
to loose the bonds of injustice,
to undo the thongs of the yoke,
to let the oppressed go free,
and to break every yoke?
Is it not to share your bread with the hungry,

and bring the homeless poor into your house;
when you see the naked, to cover them,
and not to hide yourself from your own kin?
Then your light shall break forth like the dawn,
and your healing shall spring up quickly;
your vindicator shall go before you,
the glory of the Lord shall be your rear guard.
Then you shall call, and the Lord will answer;
you shall cry for help, and he will say, Here I
    am.

Silent or spoken reflection on the readings

Song
Longing for light (SJ54)
The Lord is my light (SJ97)
Here I am (SJ100)

Zechariah's song

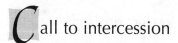all to intercession

Rejoice in the Lord always.
The Lord is near.
Do not worry about anything,
but in everything with thanksgiving
let your requests be made known to God.

God of justice, we bring our prayers to you as acts of love for you and for our neighbors.
In your mercy, Lord, hear our prayer.

You do not leave us alone. We pray for ourselves and those dear to us.
(open prayers)
You answer our pleas for help, Lord;
hear our prayer.

You do not despise or look away from the poverty of the poor. We pray for our community and for our neighbors.
(open prayers)
You answer our pleas for help, Lord;
hear our prayer.

You answer when your people cry to you. We pray for the church in all places, that we may speak boldly for Christ.
(open prayers)
You answer our pleas for help, Lord;
hear our prayer.

You prepare a banquet for all peoples. We pray for the world, for all who do justice and love mercy.
(open prayers)
You answer our pleas for help, Lord;
hear our prayer.

We offer you other concerns we carry in our
hearts.
(open prayers)
You answer our pleas for help, Lord;
hear our prayer.

God whose grace touches us
in our unworthiness,
you come near and speak the healing word.
Reveal to us this day a sign of your glory,
that we might listen to your voice
and walk in your ways.
Through Jesus our Lord,
who taught us to pray:

Our Father ...

Benediction
The Lord will guide us continually,
and satisfy our needs in parched places,
and we shall be like a watered garden,
like a spring of water,
whose waters never fail. Amen.

The oppressed go free

Opening sentences

Jesus unrolled the scroll
and found the place where it was written:
"The Spirit of the Lord is upon me
because he has anointed me
to bring good news to the poor.
He has sent me
to proclaim release to the captives
and recovery of sight to the blind,
to let the oppressed go free."

*C*all to praise

O God, your word is a lamp to my feet
and a light to my path.
The light and peace of Jesus Christ be with us.

Glory ...

Psalm 22.20-25 [19-24]

O Lord, do not leave me alone,
my strength, make haste to help me!
Rescue my soul from the sword,
my life from the grip of these dogs.
Save my life from the jaws of these lions,
my soul from the horns of these oxen.

I will tell of your name to my people
and praise you where they are assembled.
"You who fear the LORD give praise;
all children of Jacob, give glory.
Revere God, children of Israel.

For God has never despised
nor scorned the poverty of the poor,
nor looked away from them,
but has heard the poor when they cried."

Thanksgiving

It is good to give thanks to the Lord,
to sing praises to your name, O Most High.
(*free prayers of thanksgiving*)
We declare your steadfast love in the morning,
and your faithfulness by night. Amen.

Song

O worship the King (H66)
We would extol thee (H74)
O praise the gracious power (H111, vv. 1, 3, 5, 7)

Confession

Have mercy on me, O God,
according to your steadfast love;
according to your abundant mercy
blot out my transgressions.
(*silence*)
Create in me a clean heart, O God,
and put a new and right spirit within me.

Restore to me the joy of your salvation
and sustain in me a willing spirit. Amen.

Call to discipleship

Jesus said, I am the bread of life.
Whoever comes to me will never be hungry,
and whoever believes in me
will never be thirsty.
Lord Jesus, you have the words of eternal life.

Matthew 8.5-13

When [Jesus] entered Capernaum, a centurion
came to him, appealing to him and saying,
"Lord, my servant is lying at home paralyzed,
in terrible distress." And he said to him,
"I will come and cure him." The centurion
answered, "Lord, I am not worthy to have you
come under my roof; but only speak the word,
and my servant will be healed. For I also am
a man under authority, with soldiers under
me; and I say to one, 'Go,' and he goes, and
to another, 'Come,' and he comes, and to my
slave, 'Do this,' and the slave does it." When
Jesus heard him, he was amazed and said to
those who followed him, "Truly I tell you, in
no one in Israel have I found such faith. I tell
you, many will come from east and west and
will eat with Abraham and Isaac and Jacob in

the kingdom of heaven, while the heirs of the kingdom will be thrown into the outer darkness, where there will be weeping and gnashing of teeth." And to the centurion Jesus said, "Go; let it be done for you according to your faith." And the servant was healed in that hour.

Romans 1.16-17

For I am not ashamed of the gospel; it is the power of God for salvation to everyone who has faith, to the Jew first and also to the Greek. For in it the righteousness of God is revealed through faith for faith; as it is written, "The one who is righteous will live by faith."

Silent or spoken reflection on the readings

Song

Healer of our every ill (H377)
Christian, do you hear the Lord? (H494)
We walk by faith (H570)

Mary's *or* Simeon's song

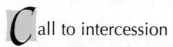 all to intercession

Ask, and it will be given you;
search, and you will find;

knock, and the door will be opened for you.
***The heavenly Father will give the Holy Spirit
to those who ask.***

God of justice, we bring our prayers to you
with confidence, in the name of our Lord
Jesus.
In your mercy, Lord, hear our prayer.

You do not leave us alone. We pray for ourselves and those dear to us.
(open prayers)
You answer our pleas for help, Lord;
hear our prayer.

You do not despise or look away from the
poverty of the poor. We pray for our community and for our neighbors.
(open prayers)
You answer our pleas for help, Lord;
hear our prayer.

You answer when your people cry to you. We
pray for the church in all places, that we may
speak boldly for Christ.
(open prayers)
You answer our pleas for help, Lord;
hear our prayer.

You prepare a banquet for all peoples. We
pray for the world, for all who do justice and
love mercy.

(open prayers)
You answer our pleas for help, Lord;
hear our prayer.

We offer you other concerns we carry in our
hearts.
(open prayers)
You answer our pleas for help, Lord;
hear our prayer.

Wondrous God,
who raised Jesus from death to life,
you heal the wounds that our swords inflict
and deliver us from fear to faith.
Grant us trust in your saving power,
that we might know your restoring touch
this night
and rise tomorrow to sing your praise.
Through Jesus the Savior,
in whose name we pray:

Our Father …

Benediction
*May God, who supplies seed to the sower
and bread for food,
supply and multiply our seed for sowing
and increase the harvest of our righteousness.
Amen.*

The year of the Lord's favor

WEEK 4 SIGNS AND WONDERS

Opening sentences

Jesus unrolled the scroll
and found the place where it was written:
"The Spirit of the Lord is upon me
because he has anointed me
to bring good news to the poor.
He has sent me
to proclaim release to the captives
and recovery of sight to the blind,
to let the oppressed go free,
to proclaim the year of the Lord's favor."

Call to praise

Lord, open our lips
and our mouths will proclaim your praise.
You are good to those who wait for you,
to all who seek you.

Glory ...

Isaiah 61.1-3

The spirit of the Lord GOD is upon me,
because the LORD has anointed me;

he has sent me to bring good news to the
  oppressed,
to bind up the brokenhearted,
to proclaim liberty to the captives,
and release to the prisoners;
to proclaim the year of the L*ORD's favor,*
and the day of vengeance of our God;
to comfort all who mourn;
to provide for those who mourn in Zion—
to give them a garland instead of ashes,
the oil of gladness instead of mourning,
the mantle of praise instead of a faint spirit.

Thanksgiving

My heart is ready, O God;
I will sing your praise.
Your steadfast love is higher than the heavens,
and your faithfulness reaches to the clouds.
(free prayers of thanksgiving)
Be exalted, O God, above the heavens,
and let your glory shine over all the earth.
Amen.

Song

Away with our fears (H292)
Jesus shall reign (H319)
He came down (SJ31)

*C*all to discipleship

Jesus said, Let anyone with ears to hear listen.
You shall love the Lord your God
with all your heart, and with all your soul,
and with all your strength,
and with all your mind;
and your neighbor as yourself.
Do this, and you will live.
Lord Jesus, you have the words of eternal life.

John 11.38-44

Then Jesus, again greatly disturbed, came to
the tomb. It was a cave, and a stone was lying
against it. Jesus said, "Take away the stone."
Martha, the sister of the dead man, said to
him, "Lord, already there is a stench because
he has been dead four days." Jesus said to her,
"Did I not tell you that if you believed, you
would see the glory of God?" So they took
away the stone. And Jesus looked upward
and said, "Father, I thank you for having
heard me. I knew that you always hear me,
but I have said this for the sake of the crowd
standing here, so that they may believe that
you sent me." When he had said this, he cried
with a loud voice, "Lazarus, come out!" The
dead man came out, his hands and feet bound
with strips of cloth, and his face wrapped in

a cloth. Jesus said to them, "Unbind him, and let him go."

1 Corinthians 15.54-57

When this perishable body puts on imperishability, and this mortal body puts on immortality, then the saying that is written will be fulfilled:

> "Death has been swallowed up in victory."
> "Where, O death, is your victory?
> Where, O death, is your sting?"

The sting of death is sin, and the power of sin is the law. But thanks be to God, who gives us the victory through our Lord Jesus Christ.

Silent or spoken reflection on the readings

Song

I know that my Redeemer lives (H277, 279)
Lift your glad voices (H275)
Thine is the glory (H269)

Zechariah's song

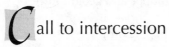

Call to intercession

Rejoice in the Lord always.
The Lord is near.

Do not worry about anything,
but in everything with thanksgiving
let your requests be made known to God.

God of resurrection and renewal, we bring our
prayers to you as acts of love for you and for
our neighbors.
In your mercy, Lord, hear our prayer.

You bring new life even where hope has died.
We pray for ourselves and those dear to us.
(open prayers)
We look to you in hope, Lord;
hear our prayer.

Your word breaks all chains. We pray for our
community and for our neighbors.
(open prayers)
We look to you in hope, Lord;
hear our prayer.

You give the oil of gladness and the mantle of
praise to your people. We pray for the church
in all places, that we may be faithful in solidarity across generations and geography.
(open prayers)
We look to you in hope, Lord;
hear our prayer.

Your gospel is the power of salvation to all.
We pray for the world, for our enemies and
for those who are in conflict.

(open prayers)
We look to you in hope, Lord;
hear our prayer.

We offer you other concerns we carry in our
hearts.
(open prayers)
We look to you in hope, Lord;
hear our prayer.

God whose grace touches us
in our unworthiness,
you come near and speak the healing word.
Reveal to us this day a sign of your glory,
that we might listen to your voice
and walk in your ways.
Through Jesus our Lord,
who taught us to pray:

Our Father …

Benediction
May the God of peace sanctify us entirely;
and may our spirit and soul and body
be kept sound and blameless
at the coming of our Lord Jesus Christ.
The one who calls us is faithful
and will do this. Amen.

The year of the Lord's favor

WEEK 4 SIGNS AND WONDERS

Opening sentences

Jesus unrolled the scroll and found
the place where it was written:
"The Spirit of the Lord is upon me
because he has anointed me
to bring good news to the poor.
He has sent me
to proclaim release to the captives
and recovery of sight to the blind,
to let the oppressed go free,
to proclaim the year of the Lord's favor."

*C*all to praise

O God, your word is a lamp to my feet
and a light to my path.
The light and peace of Jesus Christ be with us.

Glory ...

Isaiah 65.17-19, (20-23), 24-25

For I am about to create new heavens
and a new earth;
the former things shall not be remembered
or come to mind.

But be glad and rejoice forever
in what I am creating;
for I am about to create Jerusalem as a joy,
and its people as a delight.
I will rejoice in Jerusalem,
and delight in my people;
no more shall the sound of weeping be heard
    in it,
or the cry of distress.

Before they call I will answer,
while they are yet speaking I will hear.
The wolf and the lamb shall feed together,
the lion shall eat straw like the ox;
but the serpent—its food shall be dust!
They shall not hurt or destroy
*on all my holy mountain, says the L*ORD.

Thanksgiving

It is good to give thanks to the Lord,
to sing praises to your name, O Most High.
(free prayers of thanksgiving)
We declare your steadfast love in the morning,
and your faithfulness by night. Amen.

Song

New earth, heavens new (H299)
Songs of praise the angels sang (H60)
Blessed Savior, we adore thee (H107)

Confession

Have mercy on me, O God,
according to your steadfast love;
according to your abundant mercy
blot out my transgressions.
(silence)
Create in me a clean heart, O God,
and put a new and right spirit within me.
Restore to me the joy of your salvation
and sustain in me a willing spirit. Amen.

Call to discipleship

Jesus said, I am the bread of life.
Whoever comes to me will never be hungry,
and whoever believes in me
will never be thirsty.
Lord Jesus, you have the words of eternal life.

Luke 8.41-42, 49-55

There came a man named Jairus, a leader
of the synagogue. He fell at Jesus' feet and
begged him to come to his house, for he had
an only daughter, about twelve years old, who
was dying.

While he was still speaking, someone came
from the leader's house to say, "Your daughter is dead; do not trouble the teacher any longer." When Jesus heard this, he replied, "Do

not fear. Only believe, and she will be saved."
When he came to the house, he did not allow
anyone to enter with him, except Peter, John,
and James, and the child's father and mother.
They were all weeping and wailing for her;
but he said, "Do not weep; for she is not
dead but sleeping." And they laughed at him,
knowing that she was dead. But he took her
by the hand and called out, "Child, get up!"
Her spirit returned, and she got up at once.
Then he directed them to give her something
to eat.

Revelation 22.1-5

Then the angel showed me [John] the river
of the water of life, bright as crystal, flow-
ing from the throne of God and of the Lamb
through the middle of the street of the city. On
either side of the river is the tree of life with
its twelve kinds of fruit, producing its fruit
each month; and the leaves of the tree are for
the healing of the nations. Nothing accursed
will be found there any more. But the throne
of God and of the Lamb will be in it, and his
servants will worship him; they will see his
face, and his name will be on their foreheads.
And there will be no more night; they need
no light of lamp or sun, for the Lord God will
be their light, and they will reign forever and
ever.

Silent or spoken reflection on the readings

Song

Here from all nations (H296)
Oh, holy city seen of John (H320)
Oh, have you not heard (H606)

Mary's *or* Simeon's song

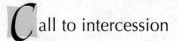

*C*all to intercession

Ask, and it will be given you;
search, and you will find;
knock, and the door will be opened for you.
The heavenly Father will give the Holy Spirit
to those who ask.

God of resurrection and renewal, we bring our
prayers to you with confidence, in the name
of our Lord Jesus.
In your mercy, Lord, hear our prayer.

You bring new life even where hope has died.
We pray for ourselves and those dear to us.
(open prayers)
We look to you in hope, Lord;
hear our prayer.

Your word breaks all chains. We pray for our
community and for our neighbors.
(open prayers)

We look to you in hope, Lord;
hear our prayer.

You give the oil of gladness and the mantle of praise to your people. We pray for the church in all places, that we may be faithful in solidarity across generations and geography.
(open prayers)
We look to you in hope, Lord;
hear our prayer.

Your gospel is the power of salvation to all. We pray for the world, for our enemies and for those who are in conflict.
(open prayers)
We look to you in hope, Lord;
hear our prayer.

We offer you other concerns we carry in our hearts.
(open prayers)
We look to you in hope, Lord;
hear our prayer.

Wondrous God,
who raised Jesus from death to life,
you heal the wounds that our swords inflict
and deliver us from fear to faith.
Grant us trust in your saving power,
that we might know your restoring touch
this night
and rise tomorrow to sing your praise.

Through Jesus the Savior,
in whose name we pray:

Our Father ...

Benediction
*May the Lord direct our hearts
to the love of God
and to the steadfastness of Christ. Amen.*

Appendix: Additional songs

WEEK 1: LORD'S PRAYER

Sunday morning
praise
Praise, praise, praise the Lord! (SJ11)
Who is so great a God (H62)
For the beauty of the earth (H89)

after readings
Mayenziwe (Your will be done) (SJ57)
Holy Spirit, truth divine (H508, SS105)
Our Father, which art in heaven (SS42)

Sunday evening
praise
O bless the Lord, my soul (H80)
Our Father God, thy name we praise (H32)
Santo (Holy) (SJ15)

after readings
There are many gifts (H304)
I know that my Redeemer lives (H277)

Monday morning
praise
The Lord is King (H69)
Alleluia (H101)
Before Jehovah's aweful throne (H18)
Praise, my soul, the God of heaven (H63)

after readings
If you believe and I believe (SJ32)
Jesus, help us live in peace (SJ52)

Monday evening
praise

after readings
My soul cries out (SS124)
Our Father, which art in heaven (SJ48)
Our Father who art in heaven (H228)
Our Father, which art in heaven (SS42)

Tuesday morning
praise
Now thank we all our God (H85, 86)
I sing the mighty power of God (H46)

after readings
I will come to you in the silence (SS49)
I hunger and I thirst (H474)

Tuesday evening
praise
O Holy Spirit, by whose breath (H291)
Still, I search for my God (H88)
Oh, that I had a thousand voices (H84)

after readings
Nothing is lost (SS121)
Sometimes a light surprises (H603)
Let the hungry come to me (H464, vv. 1-3)
Our Father, which art in heaven (SJ48)
Our Father who art in heaven (H228)
Our Father, which art in heaven (SS42)

Wednesday morning
praise
When all thy mercies, O my God (H72)
Praise with joy the world's Creator (SJ16)

after readings
Where charity and love prevail (H305)
Christ, from whom all blessings (H365)
Slowly turning, ever turning (SJ23)

Wednesday evening

praise
Praise the Lord who reigns above (H54)
O come, loud anthems let us sing (H68)
Halle, halle, hallelujah! (SJ17)
I love thy kingdom, Lord (H308)

after readings
O God in heaven (SJ53)
Oh, Lord have mercy (SJ47)
Just as I am, without one plea (H516, SJ92)
Our Father, which art in heaven (SJ48)
Our Father who art in heaven (H228)
Our Father, which art in heaven (SS42)

Thursday morning

praise
Great God, how infinite art thou! (H82)
Ehane he'ama (Father God, you are holy) (H78)

after readings
When the storms of life are raging (H558)
Nada te turbe (H562)
La ténèbre (Our darkness) (SJ101)
In the morning when I rise (SJ45)
Jesus walked this lonesome valley (SS80)

Thursday evening

praise

after readings
Wehrlos und verlassen sehnt sich (SJ93)
O God, to whom then shall I turn (SS61)
We are often tossed and driven (SS72)
Our Father, which art in heaven (SJ48)
Our Father who art in heaven (H228)
Our Father, which art in heaven (SS42)

Friday morning

praise
Alleluia (SJ41)
I to the hills will lift my eyes (H169, 563)
Great is thy faithfulness (H327)

after readings
Lord Jesus, think on me (H527)

Friday evening

praise
I am trusting thee, Lord Jesus (H564)
Alleluia (H101)

after readings
Guide my feet (H546)
Our Father, which art in heaven (SJ48)
Our Father who art in heaven (H228)
Our Father, which art in heaven (SS42)

Saturday morning

praise
All hail the power of Jesus' name (H106, 285)

after readings
You are salt for the earth (H226)
Jesus shall reign (H319)

Saturday evening

praise

after readings
Awake, my soul (H609)

WEEK 2: BEATITUDES

Sunday morning

praise
Each morning brings us (H645)
We sing to you, O God (SJ1)

after readings
Prince of peace, control my will (H534)
Like a mother who has borne us (SJ91)

Sunday evening

praise
Keep me safe, O God (SJ50)

after readings
How bless'd are they (H525)
My faith has found a resting place (SJ43)
Blessed are they (SS41)

Monday morning

praise

after readings

Monday evening

praise
When all thy mercies, O my God (H72)
I will call upon the Lord (SJ19)

after readings
Blest are they (SJ94)
Blessed are the persecuted (H230)

Tuesday morning

praise
I owe my Lord a morning song (SJ112)

after readings
Oh, blessed are the poor in spirit (H231)

Tuesday evening
praise
God of our strength (H36)

after readings
Blest are they (SJ94)

Wednesday morning
praise

after readings
Where charity and love prevail (H305)
Christ, from whom all blessings (H365)
Slowly turning, ever turning (SJ23)

Wednesday evening
praise
Great is the Lord (H87)
Sing praise to God who reigns (H59)

after readings
Blest are they (SJ94)

Thursday morning
praise
Come, my Way, my Truth, my Life (H587)

after readings
Where charity and love prevail (H305)

Thursday evening
praise
All people that on earth do dwell (H42)
Praise to the Lord, the Almighty (H37)
Creating God, your fingers trace (H325)

after readings
How bless'd are they (H525)
Beloved, God's chosen (SJ38)
Oh, blessed are the poor in spirit (H231)

Friday morning

praise
Santo, santo, santo (Holy, holy, holy) (H400)

after readings
How can we be silent (SJ61)
Peace before us (SS16)

Friday evening

praise
Here in this place (H6)
Create my soul anew (H3)

after readings
Come, Holy Spirit, descend (SJ33)
Dona nobis pacem (H346)
Spirit, working in creation (SJ10)
Blest are they (SJ94)

Saturday morning

praise
Gloria (H204)

after readings
O Jesus Christ, may grateful hymns (H404)

Saturday evening

praise
The Lord is my light (SJ97)
A mighty fortress is our God (H165)

after readings
How firm a foundation (H567)
Blest are they (SJ94)

WEEK 3: PARABLES

Sunday morning

praise

Praise, my soul, the King of heaven (H65)
There's a wideness in God's mercy (H145)
Lord, with devotion we pray (H79)
Oh, how wondrous the grace (H147)

after readings

Ah, what shame I have to bear (H531)
Christ, we do all adore thee (H105)
When in the hour of deepest need (H131)
Kyrie eleison (H144)
Kyrie Eleison (SS68)

Sunday evening

praise

From time beyond my memory (H484)
My life flows on (H580)

after readings

Wonderful grace of Jesus (H150)
In your sickness (H585)
How firm a foundation (H567)
O Love that will not let me go (H577)
Jesus, priceless treasure (H595)
Christ be near at either hand (SJ80)

Monday morning

praise

As rain from the clouds (SJ40)
From the hands (H97)
Praise to God, immortal praise (H91)
God, whose farm is all creation (H391)

after readings

How clear is our vocation, Lord (H541)
Savior of my soul (H549)
Take, O take me as I am (SJ81)

Monday evening
praise
The God of Abraham praise (H162)

after readings

Tuesday morning
praise
How bless'd are they (H525)

after readings
O Lamb of God all holy! (H146)
Lamb of God (SJ21)

Tuesday evening
praise
Praise, praise, praise the Lord! (SJ11)
When the morning stars together (H34)

after readings
God of the Bible (SJ27)
Jesus Christ is waiting (SJ30)
How can we be silent (SJ61)

Wednesday morning
praise
O God, our help in ages past (H328)
From all that dwell below the skies (H49)
Lord, with devotion we pray (H79)

after readings

Wednesday evening
praise
Glorious things of thee are spoken (H619)
Come, we that love the Lord (H14)

after readings
Cuando el pobre (When the poor ones) (SJ69)
Where cross the crowded ways (H405)
The church of Christ, in every age (H403)

Thursday morning
praise
Forth in thy name (H415)

after readings

Thursday evening
praise
How bless'd are they (H525)

after readings
Sleepers, wake (H188)

Friday morning
praise
Out of the depths I cry to you (H133)
O God, who gives us life (H483)
I to the hills will lift mine eyes (H563)
I to the hills will lift my eyes (H169)

after readings
Rejoice, the Lord is King (H288)

Friday evening
praise
Alleluia (SJ41)

after readings
In the bulb there is a flower (H614)
Have thine own way (H504)

Saturday morning
praise
The King of love my shepherd is (H170)
Lord, thou hast searched me (H556)
When long before time (SJ25)

after readings
Marvelous grace of our loving Lord (H151)

Saturday evening

praise
When in the hour of deepest need (H131)
O Love of God (H326)
I will call upon the Lord (SJ19)

after readings
Taste and see (SJ86)
Here from all nations (H296)

WEEK 4: SIGNS AND WONDERS

Sunday morning
praise

after readings
O Breath of Life (SJ35)

Sunday evening
praise
Proclaim the tidings near and far (H282)
Lift your glad voices (H275)
Cantai ao Senhor (O sing to the Lord) (SJ12)

after readings
Don't be afraid (SJ105)
Come, Holy Spirit, descend (SJ33)
O Breath of Life (SJ35)

Monday morning
praise
The God of Abraham praise (H162)
O thou, in whose presence (H559)

after readings

Monday evening

praise
Halle, halle, hallelujah! (SJ17)
Praise God from whom (H119)

after readings
Taste and see (SJ86)

Tuesday morning

praise
O Jesus Christ, may grateful hymns (H404)
Creator of the stars of night (H177)
Praise him, praise him (H100)

after readings
Christian, do you hear the Lord? (H494)
Healer of our every ill (H377)

Tuesday evening

praise
Sing praise to God who reigns (H59)
My soul is filled with joy (SJ13)

after readings
Ask ye what great thing I know (H337)
I know not why God's wondrous (H338)
Immortal love, forever full (H629)

Wednesday morning

praise
Longing for light (SJ54)

after readings
In your sickness (H585)
I am weak and I need thy strength (H553)
Here I am (SJ100)

Wednesday evening

praise
Santo, santo, santo (Holy, holy, holy) (H400)
Praise, my soul, the King of heaven (H65)
Now thank we all our God (H86)

after readings
Oh, Lord have mercy (SJ47)
Oh, have you not heard (H606)
Oh, for a thousand tongues to sing (H110)

Thursday morning

praise
Great is the Lord (H87)
Asithi: Amen (Sing amen) (H64)

after readings
Abre mis ojos (Open my eyes) (SS65)

Thursday evening

praise
Praise, praise, praise the Lord! (SJ11)
O Lord, our Lord, how majestic (H112)

after readings
Listen, God is calling (SJ42)

Friday morning

praise
In the rifted Rock I'm resting (H526)
Thy holy wings (SJ118)

after readings
Lord, whose love in humble service (H369)

Friday evening

praise
Praise with joy the world's Creator (SJ16)
In thee is gladness (H114)

after readings

Saturday morning

praise

The church of Christ, in every age (H403)
Santo, santo, santo (Holy, holy, holy) (H400)

after readings

I am the Bread of life (H472)
Christ is arisen (H271)

Saturday evening

praise

God of many names (H77)
Praise God from whom (H118)
Sing praise to God who reigns (H59)

after readings

Crown him with many crowns (H116)
Christ, we do all adore thee (H105)
I want to walk as a child of the light (SJ95)

Scripture index:
Readings and Psalms

This scripture index includes entries for both Volume 1 (*Ordinary Time*) and Volume 2 (*Advent through Pentecost*) of *Take Our Moments and Our Days: An Anabaptist Prayer Book.*

Joshua

24.14-15	Christmas 2	Jan 5	morning	Reading 2
	Holy week	Thursday	evening	Reading 1

1 Samuel

2.1-10	Advent	Wednesday	morning	Reading 2
24.16-20	Holy week	Tuesday	morning	Reading 1

1 Kings

17.8-16	Ordinary 1	Tuesday	evening	Reading 2
19.9-12	Epiphany	Saturday	evening	Reading 2

2 Kings

4.42-44	Ordinary 4	Monday	evening	Reading 2

1 Chronicles

16.23-31	Epiphany	Friday	morning	Psalm

Nehemiah

9.5-8	Epiphany	Monday	evening	Psalm

Esther

4.12-16	Lent	Friday	morning	Reading 2

Job

31.13-23	Holy week	Wednesday	evening	Psalm

Psalms

1	Lent	Tuesday	morning	Psalm
	Pentecost 2	Sunday	morning	Psalm
2	Easter	Tuesday	morning	Psalm
2.1-8	Epiphany	Saturday	evening	Psalm
8	Holy week	Wednesday	morning	Psalm
10.12-18	Ordinary 4	Tuesday	evening	Psalm
13	Holy week	Saturday	evening	Psalm
15	Lent	Wednesday	morning	Psalm
16.7-11	Epiphany	Wednesday	evening	Psalm
	Pentecost	Wednesday	morning	Psalm
17	Holy week	Saturday	morning	Psalm
19.7-9	Ordinary 3	Monday	evening	Psalm
19.7-14	Pentecost 2	Wednesday	evening	Psalm
20.1-8	Ordinary 4	Sunday	morning	Psalm
22.1-8	Holy week	Friday	morning	Psalm
22.9-21	Holy week	Friday	evening	Psalm

22.19-24	Ordinary 4	Friday	evening	Psalm
24.1-6	Ordinary 2	Thursday	evening	Psalm
25.1-7	Ordinary 3	Friday	morning	Psalm
25.8-14	Ordinary 2	Tuesday	evening	Psalm
25.16-21	Ordinary 1	Thursday	morning	Psalm
26	Holy week	Thursday	evening	Psalm
27	Holy week	Thursday	morning	Psalm
29	Epiphany	Tuesday	morning	Psalm
30.2-5	Ordinary 2	Monday	evening	Psalm
31.9-15	Ordinary 1	Thursday	evening	Psalm
31.19-24	Ordinary 2	Saturday	morning	Psalm
32.1-5	Ordinary 3	Sunday	morning	Psalm
33.1-5	Ordinary 3	Tuesday	evening	Psalm
34.11-18	Ordinary 2	Friday	evening	Psalm
36.5-9	Ordinary 2	Wednesday	morning	Psalm
37.3-11	Ordinary 2	Tuesday	morning	Psalm
41	Holy week	Tuesday	evening	Psalm
43	Ordinary 2	Saturday	evening	Psalm
	Lent	Sunday	evening	Psalm
46	Lent	Saturday	evening	Psalm
47	Easter	Thursday	morning	Psalm
48.9-14	Ordinary 3	Wednesday	evening	Psalm
50.1-6	Epiphany	Sunday	evening	Psalm
51.1-12	Lent	Monday	morning	Psalm
51.6-13	Pentecost	Friday	evening	Psalm
51.12-17	Ordinary 3	Tuesday	morning	Psalm
53	Lent	Tuesday	evening	Psalm
61.1-5	Ordinary 4	Friday	morning	Psalm
65.1-4	Ordinary 1	Wednesday	evening	Psalm
65.9-13	Ordinary 3	Monday	morning	Psalm
66.1-9	Ordinary 4	Monday	evening	Psalm
67	Epiphany	Thursday	evening	Psalm
68.4-12	Christmas 1	Dec 24	evening	Psalm
68.17-20	Pentecost	Friday	morning	Psalm
71.1-4	Ordinary 1	Friday	evening	Psalm
71.5-8	Ordinary 3	Saturday	morning	Psalm
71.15-19	Ordinary 3	Friday	evening	Psalm
72.12-14	Ordinary 4	Tuesday	morning	Psalm
75	Lent	Thursday	morning	Psalm

77.4-15	Epiphany	Tuesday	evening	Psalm
78.18-26	Ordinary 1	Tuesday	morning	Psalm
82	Lent	Sunday	morning	Psalm
84	Lent	Thursday	evening	Psalm
85.1-7	Christmas 1	Dec 29	morning	Psalm
85.7-13	Ordinary 2	Friday	morning	Psalm
86.1-8	Ordinary 2	Thursday	morning	Psalm
90.11-14	Christmas 2	Dec 31	morning	Psalm
90.15-17	Christmas 2	Jan 1	evening	Psalm
91	Lent	Friday	morning	Psalm
91.1-6	Christmas 2	Jan 2	morning	Psalm
91.8-17	Christmas 2	Jan 2	evening	Psalm
95.1-7	Christmas 2	Jan 3	morning	Psalm
	Easter	Monday	evening	Psalm
96	Christmas 1	Dec 25	evening	Psalm
96.9-13	Easter	Saturday	evening	Psalm
96.10-13	Ordinary 2	Wednesday	evening	Psalm
97	Easter	Wednesday	evening	Psalm
97.1-6	Christmas 2	Jan 4	evening	Psalm
97.6-12	Christmas 1	Dec 29	evening	Psalm
98	Easter	Thursday	evening	Psalm
98.1-4	Christmas 2	Jan 5	morning	Psalm
99	Easter	Friday	evening	Psalm
99.1-5	Ordinary 1	Monday	morning	Psalm
100	Easter	Tuesday	evening	Psalm
101	Lent	Wednesday	evening	Psalm
102.15-22	Christmas 1	Dec 27	morning	Psalm
102.24-28	Christmas 2	Jan 1	morning	Psalm
103.1-7	Ordinary 1	Sunday	evening	Psalm
103.6-14	Christmas 2	Dec 31	evening	Psalm
103.8-14	Ordinary 1	Wednesday	morning	Psalm
103.19-22	Ordinary 1	Monday	evening	Psalm
104.1-4, 10-15	Ordinary 1	Sunday	morning	Psalm
104.27-30	Ordinary 1	Tuesday	evening	Psalm
105.1-5, 40-43	Ordinary 4	Monday	morning	Psalm
107.10-16	Ordinary 4	Wednesday	morning	Psalm
110.1-4	Easter	Sunday	evening	Psalm
111.1-4	Ordinary 4	Thursday	morning	Psalm
114	Christmas 1	Dec 28	morning	Psalm

116.2-9	Ordinary 3	Saturday	evening	Psalm
118.13-17	Ordinary 4	Sunday	evening	Psalm
118.14-29	Easter	Sunday	morning	Psalm
118.19-29	Holy week	Sunday	morning	Psalm
119.1-8	Pentecost 2	Sunday	evening	Psalm
119.9-16	Pentecost 2	Monday	morning	Psalm
119.17-24	Pentecost 2	Monday	evening	Psalm
119.33-40	Pentecost 2	Tuesday	morning	Psalm
119.41-48	Holy week	Sunday	evening	Psalm
119.49-56	Holy week	Monday	morning	Psalm
119.57-64	Ordinary 3	Thursday	morning	Psalm
	Holy week	Monday	evening	Psalm
119.73-80	Pentecost 2	Tuesday	evening	Psalm
119.89-96	Pentecost 2	Wednesday	morning	Psalm
119.97-104	Pentecost 2	Thursday	morning	Psalm
119.113-120	Pentecost 2	Thursday	evening	Psalm
119.129-136	Ordinary 3	Thursday	evening	Psalm
	Pentecost 2	Friday	morning	Psalm
119.145-152	Pentecost 2	Friday	evening	Psalm
119.161-168	Pentecost 2	Saturday	morning	Psalm
119.169-176	Pentecost 2	Saturday	evening	Psalm
126	Ordinary 2	Monday	morning	Psalm
131.1-2	Ordinary 2	Sunday	evening	Psalm
133	Epiphany	Wednesday	morning	Psalm
135.1-7	Christmas 2	Jan 4	morning	Psalm
136.1-9	Christmas 2	Jan 3	evening	Psalm
138.1-5	Epiphany	Thursday	morning	Psalm
139.1-6	Ordinary 3	Sunday	evening	Psalm
139.13-18	Epiphany	Sunday	morning	Psalm
140.1-7	Ordinary 1	Friday	morning	Psalm
143.5-10	Pentecost	Wednesday	evening	Psalm
145.1-9	Ordinary 1	Saturday	evening	Psalm
145.1-13, 21	Easter	Saturday	morning	Psalm
145.10-14	Ordinary 1	Saturday	morning	Psalm
145.15-21	Ordinary 3	Wednesday	morning	Psalm
146	Lent	Saturday	morning	Psalm
146.1-9	Ordinary 4	Thursday	evening	Psalm
147.1-7	Ordinary 4	Wednesday	evening	Psalm
148	Easter	Friday	morning	Psalm

| 150 | Christmas 2 | Jan 5 | evening | Psalm |

Song of Solomon

| 8.6-7 | Holy week | Saturday | morning | Reading 1 |

Isaiah

2.1-5	Holy week	Tuesday	morning	Psalm
2.2-4	Epiphany	Friday	evening	Psalm
6.1-8	Epiphany	Thursday	evening	Reading 1
7.14-15	Advent	Wednesday	evening	Psalm
9.1-5	Christmas 1	Dec 30	morning	Psalm
9.2-7	Advent	Thursday	morning	Psalm
9.6-7	Christmas 1	Dec 30	evening	Psalm
11.1-9	Advent	Wednesday	morning	Psalm
11.1-4a, 10-12				
	Pentecost	Monday	morning	Psalm
11.6-9	Easter	Wednesday	morning	Psalm
12.1-2	Christmas 1	Dec 27	evening	Reading 2
12.2-6	Advent	Tuesday	morning	Psalm
25.6-9	Ordinary 3	Saturday	evening	Reading 2
25.9	Christmas 2	Jan 4	evening	Reading 2
30.18-21	Christmas 1	Dec 26	evening	Psalm
32.15-18	Ordinary 2	Friday	evening	Reading 2
35.1-6	Advent	Sunday	evening	Psalm
40.1-2	Ordinary 2	Monday	evening	Reading 2
40.3	Christmas 2	Jan 2	evening	Reading 2
40.9-11	Advent	Thursday	evening	Psalm
42.1-6	Pentecost	Tuesday	evening	Psalm
42.6-9	Christmas 1	Dec 26	evening	Reading 2
43.1-3	Epiphany	Saturday	morning	Psalm
43.15-21	Advent	Tuesday	evening	Psalm
49.1-6	Epiphany	Monday	morning	Psalm
49.6	Christmas 1	Dec 27	morning	Reading 2
49.8-11	Advent	Friday	morning	Psalm
49.13-15	Christmas 1	Dec 28	morning	Reading 2
52.7-10	Advent	Sunday	morning	Psalm
	Pentecost	Sunday	evening	Psalm
52.10-15	Lent	Friday	evening	Psalm
53.1-9	Lent	Monday	evening	Psalm
54.11-14	Advent	Saturday	evening	Psalm

Amos

5.24	Ordinary 2	Wednesday	evening	Reading 2

Micah

4.6-10	Christmas 1	Dec 26	morning	Psalm
5.2	Christmas 1	Dec 25	evening	Reading 2
6.6-8	Ordinary 2	Wednesday	morning	Reading 2
	Lent	Saturday	morning	Reading 2

Nahum

1.15	Christmas 1	Dec 30	evening	Reading 2

Habakkuk

3.17-19	Holy week	Saturday	evening	Reading 1

Zephaniah

3.14-20	Advent	Thursday	evening	Reading 2
3.19	Holy week	Friday	evening	Reading 1

Zechariah

4.1-7	Pentecost 2	Thursday	morning	Reading 1

Malachi

2.5-6	Lent	Wednesday	evening	Reading 2
3.1-4	Advent	Friday	morning	Reading 2
4.5-6	Christmas 2	Jan 3	evening	Reading 2

Matthew

1.18-25	Advent	Wednesday	evening	Reading 1
2.1-6	Epiphany	Jan 6	morning	Reading 1
2.7-12	Epiphany	Jan 6	evening	Reading 1
2.13-15	Christmas 1	Dec 28	morning	Reading 1
2.16-18	Christmas 1	Dec 28	evening	Reading 1
2.19-23	Christmas 1	Dec 29	morning	Reading 1
4.1-7	Ordinary 1	Friday	morning	Reading 1
4.8-11	Ordinary 1	Friday	evening	Reading 1
4.12-17	Advent	Sunday	morning	Reading 1
5.20, 46-48	Ordinary 2	Wednesday	evening	Reading 1
5.38-45	Ordinary 2	Friday	morning	Reading 1
6.19-21	Christmas 2	Dec 31	morning	Reading 1
6.26-33	Christmas 2	Dec 31	evening	Reading 1
8.5-13	Ordinary 4	Friday	evening	Reading 1
10.16-20	Ordinary 2	Saturday	evening	Reading 1

12.15-20	Ordinary 4	Sunday	morning	Reading 1
13.31-33	Advent	Tuesday	evening	Reading 2
13.44-46	Ordinary 3	Friday	evening	Reading 1
17.1-8	Epiphany	Saturday	morning	Reading 1
17.9-13	Epiphany	Saturday	evening	Reading 1
18.1-5	Ordinary 2	Sunday	evening	Reading 1
20.8-16	Ordinary 3	Saturday	morning	Reading 1
21.28-31	Ordinary 3	Thursday	morning	Reading 1
25.34-40	Ordinary 3	Wednesday	evening	Reading 1
26.36-39	Ordinary 1	Thursday	morning	Reading 1
26.40-46	Ordinary 1	Thursday	evening	Reading 1
28.1-10	Easter	Sunday	morning	Reading 1

Mark

1.4-11	Epiphany	Sunday	morning	Reading 1
1.14-15	Ordinary 1	Saturday	morning	Reading 1
1.40-45	Ordinary 4	Tuesday	morning	Reading 1
3.1-6	Ordinary 4	Friday	morning	Reading 1
4.1-9	Ordinary 3	Monday	morning	Reading 1
6.39-44	Ordinary 4	Monday	evening	Reading 1
8.22-26	Ordinary 4	Thursday	evening	Reading 1
9.14-29	Ordinary 4	Wednesday	morning	Reading 1
9.33-37	Ordinary 2	Tuesday	evening	Reading 1
10.46-52	Ordinary 4	Thursday	morning	Reading 1
11.25	Ordinary 1	Wednesday	morning	Reading 1
13.32-37	Ordinary 3	Friday	morning	Reading 1
15.47-16.8	Ordinary 2	Sunday	morning	Reading 1

Luke

1.5-7	Advent	Monday	morning	Reading 1
1.8-17	Advent	Monday	evening	Reading 1
1.18-20	Advent	Tuesday	morning	Reading 1
1.21-25	Advent	Tuesday	evening	Reading 1
1.26-38	Advent	Wednesday	morning	Reading 1
1.39-45	Advent	Thursday	morning	Reading 1
1.57-67, 80	Advent	Thursday	evening	Reading 1
2.1-7	Christmas 1	Dec 24	evening	Reading 1
2.8-14	Christmas 1	Dec 25	morning	Reading 1
2.15-20	Christmas 1	Dec 25	evening	Reading 1
2.21-24	Christmas 1	Dec 26	morning	Reading 1

2.21-30	Holy week	Monday	evening	Reading 2
2.25-32	Christmas 1	Dec 26	evening	Reading 1
2.33-35	Christmas 1	Dec 27	morning	Reading 1
2.36-38	Christmas 1	Dec 27	evening	Reading 1
2.39-40	Christmas 1	Dec 29	evening	Reading 1
2.41-47	Christmas 1	Dec 30	morning	Reading 1
2.48-52	Christmas 1	Dec 30	evening	Reading 1
3.1-6	Advent	Friday	morning	Reading 1
3.7-18	Advent	Friday	evening	Reading 1
4.17-19	Lent	Sunday	morning	Reading 1
4.24-30	Lent	Sunday	evening	Reading 1
5.18-26	Lent	Monday	morning	Reading 1
6.20-26	Lent	Tuesday	morning	Reading 1
6.27-31	Lent	Thursday	morning	Reading 1
6.32-36	Lent	Thursday	evening	Reading 1
6.32-38	Ordinary 2	Thursday	morning	Reading 1
7.18-23	Advent	Sunday	evening	Reading 1
7.36-50	Lent	Tuesday	evening	Reading 1
7.40-50	Ordinary 1	Wednesday	evening	Reading 1
8.41-42, 49-55	Ordinary 4	Saturday	evening	Reading 1
8.43-48	Ordinary 4	Tuesday	evening	Reading 1
9.23-27	Lent	Friday	evening	Reading 1
9.51-56	Lent	Monday	evening	Reading 1
10.5-11	Ordinary 1	Monday	evening	Reading 1
10.29-37	Ordinary 3	Tuesday	evening	Reading 1
11.1-4, 9-13	Ordinary 1	Sunday	morning	Reading 1
12.22-31	Ordinary 1	Tuesday	evening	Reading 1
12.29-34	Lent	Friday	morning	Reading 1
12.35-40	Ordinary 3	Thursday	evening	Reading 1
13.18-21	Ordinary 3	Monday	evening	Reading 1
14.7-11	Ordinary 2	Tuesday	morning	Reading 1
14.12-14	Lent	Wednesday	morning	Reading 1
14.16-24	Ordinary 3	Saturday	evening	Reading 1
15.11-19	Ordinary 3	Sunday	morning	Reading 1
15.20-24	Ordinary 3	Sunday	evening	Reading 1
17.20-21	Ordinary 1	Monday	morning	Reading 1
18.1-8	Ordinary 3	Wednesday	morning	Reading 1
18.9-14	Ordinary 3	Tuesday	morning	Reading 1

2.37-41	Pentecost	Friday	morning	Reading 1
2.42-47	Pentecost	Saturday	morning	Reading 1
3.1-10	Advent	Sunday	evening	Reading 2
4.1-12	Easter	Monday	evening	Reading 2
4.5-14	Ordinary 4	Tuesday	morning	Reading 2
4.24-31	Ordinary 4	Sunday	morning	Reading 2
5.12-16	Ordinary 4	Wednesday	evening	Reading 2
6.1-6	Pentecost 2	Sunday	evening	Reading 1
8.14-25	Pentecost 2	Tuesday	morning	Reading 2
8.26-39	Pentecost 2	Tuesday	evening	Reading 1
9.1-9	Epiphany	Thursday	morning	Reading 2
9.10-18	Epiphany	Thursday	evening	Reading 2
9.10-20	Pentecost 2	Monday	morning	Reading 2
9.26-31	Pentecost 2	Monday	evening	Reading 1
10.34-43	Easter	Friday	evening	Reading 2
10.44-48	Pentecost	Monday	morning	Reading 2
11.11-18	Pentecost	Wednesday	morning	Reading 2
	Pentecost 2	Wednesday	morning	Reading 2
11.19-26	Pentecost 2	Wednesday	evening	Reading 1
13.1-5	Pentecost 2	Thursday	evening	Reading 1
19.1-7	Pentecost 2	Friday	morning	Reading 2
20.16-24	Pentecost 2	Saturday	morning	Reading 2
20.25-32	Pentecost 2	Saturday	evening	Reading 1
21.7-14	Pentecost 2	Friday	evening	Reading 1
22.6-15	Ordinary 4	Thursday	evening	Reading 2
26.12-18	Ordinary 4	Thursday	morning	Reading 2

Romans

1.1-6	Advent	Wednesday	evening	Reading 2
1.16-17	Ordinary 4	Friday	evening	Reading 2
2.1-11	Lent	Tuesday	evening	Reading 2
4.18-22	Epiphany	Monday	evening	Reading 2
5.1-5	Lent	Thursday	morning	Reading 2
5.6-11	Ordinary 3	Sunday	morning	Reading 2
	Lent	Thursday	evening	Reading 2
8.14-17	Pentecost	Monday	evening	Reading 2
8.31-39	Christmas 2	Dec 31	evening	Reading 2
8.35-39	Ordinary 3	Sunday	evening	Reading 2
10.9-18	Pentecost	Tuesday	morning	Reading 2
12.1-2	Ordinary 3	Friday	evening	Reading 2

12.9-16	Ordinary 2	Thursday	morning	Reading 2
13.11-14	Advent	Saturday	evening	Reading 2
14.15-17	Ordinary 1	Monday	morning	Reading 2
15.7-13	Pentecost	Sunday	morning	Reading 2
15.25-33	Pentecost	Saturday	morning	Reading 2
16.25-27	Advent	Thursday	morning	Reading 2

1 Corinthians

1.18-25	Lent	Sunday	evening	Reading 2
1.26-31	Ordinary 2	Sunday	evening	Reading 2
10.12-13	Ordinary 1	Thursday	morning	Reading 2
12.3-11	Pentecost	Thursday	morning	Reading 2
12.12-26	Lent	Tuesday	morning	Reading 2
15.54-57	Ordinary 4	Saturday	morning	Reading 2

2 Corinthians

2.5-11	Ordinary 1	Wednesday	evening	Reading 2
3.12-13, 16-18				
	Epiphany	Wednesday	evening	Reading 2
3.17-18	Ordinary 4	Sunday	evening	Reading 2
	Pentecost	Wednesday	evening	Reading 2
4.5-15	Epiphany	Friday	morning	Reading 2
4.6	Ordinary 4	Monday	morning	Reading 2
8.1-6	Pentecost 2	Sunday	evening	Reading 2
8.7-9	Pentecost 2	Monday	evening	Reading 2
8.9	Christmas 1	Dec 24	evening	Reading 2
8.10-15	Pentecost 2	Tuesday	evening	Reading 2
8.16-19	Pentecost 2	Wednesday	evening	Reading 2
8.20-24	Pentecost 2	Thursday	evening	Reading 2
9.5-7	Pentecost 2	Friday	evening	Reading 2
9.8-15	Pentecost 2	Saturday	evening	Reading 2
12.7-10	Ordinary 4	Wednesday	morning	Reading 2

Galatians

| 3.6-14 | Epiphany | Monday | morning | Reading 2 |
| 5.16-25 | Pentecost | Tuesday | evening | Reading 2 |

Ephesians

1.3-10	Christmas 1	Dec 29	morning	Reading 2
1.11-17	Pentecost	Saturday	evening	Reading 2
1.15-23	Easter	Tuesday	morning	Reading 2
1.17-23	Christmas 2	Jan 5	evening	Reading 2

James

1.12-15	Ordinary 1	Thursday	evening	Reading 2
1.22-27	Ordinary 3	Thursday	morning	Reading 2
2.1-9	Lent	Wednesday	morning	Reading 2
2.8	Ordinary 3	Tuesday	evening	Reading 2
3.13-18	Ordinary 2	Thursday	evening	Reading 2
4.5-10	Ordinary 2	Sunday	morning	Reading 2
4.13-15	Christmas 2	Dec 31	morning	Reading 2
5.7-11	Advent	Saturday	morning	Reading 2

1 Peter

1.3-9	Easter	Saturday	morning	Reading 2
1.17-23	Advent	Monday	evening	Reading 2
2.4-5	Holy week	Sunday	morning	Reading 2
3.13-16	Ordinary 2	Saturday	evening	Reading 2
4.1-6	Lent	Monday	evening	Reading 2
4.7-11	Ordinary 3	Friday	morning	Reading 2
4.12-19	Christmas 1	Dec 28	evening	Reading 2

2 Peter

| 3.8-9 | Ordinary 3 | Thursday | evening | Reading 2 |

1 John

2.29–3.2	Christmas 2	Jan 1	evening	Reading 2
3.16-24	Pentecost	Thursday	evening	Reading 2
4.7-12	Christmas 1	Dec 25	morning	Reading 2
	Lent	Friday	evening	Reading 2

Revelation

1.12-20	Epiphany	Friday	evening	Reading 2
4.9-11	Ordinary 1	Saturday	morning	Reading 2
5.1-10	Easter	Wednesday	morning	Reading 2
5.11-14	Easter	Wednesday	evening	Reading 2
5.13-14	Christmas 2	Jan 4	morning	Reading 2
7.13-17	Ordinary 2	Monday	morning	Reading 2
11.15-18	Christmas 1	Dec 30	morning	Reading 2
19.1-5	Easter	Thursday	morning	Reading 2
19.6-10	Easter	Thursday	evening	Reading 2
21.1-4	Ordinary 1	Monday	evening	Reading 2
22.1-5	Ordinary 4	Saturday	evening	Reading 2

Scripture index: Other elements

Week 2	Sunday		Heb 13.20-21
	Monday		2 Cor 1.3-5
	Tuesday		Eph 3.20-21
	Wednesday		2 Cor 9.10
	Thursday		Lk 1.78-79
	Friday	morning	1 Thes 5.23-24
		evening	Nm 6.24-26
	Saturday		1 Pet 5.10
Week 3	Sunday		Heb 13.20-21
	Monday	morning	Is 58.11
		evening	Rom 15.13
	Tuesday	morning	Col 2.2
		evening	1 Jn 2.28
	Wednesday	morning	Nm 6.24-26
		evening	2 Cor 9.10
	Thursday	morning	Col 1.10
		evening	Col 1.9
	Friday	morning	1 Pt 5.10
		evening	Lk 1.78-79
	Saturday	morning	1 Thes 5.23-24
		evening	Rom 15.5-6
Week 4	Sunday		Heb 13.20-21
	Monday	morning	Eph 3.20-21
		evening	Eph 6.23
	Tuesday	morning	2 Thes 3.5
		evening	2 Thes 3.16
	Wednesday		Jude 24-25
	Thursday		Ps 121.7-8
	Friday	morning	Is 58.11
		evening	2 Cor 9.10
	Saturday	morning	1 Thes 5.23-24
		evening	2 Thes 3.5

Musical settings of calls and responses

Lord, open our lips

CALL TO PRAISE

Lord, o - pen our lips and our mouths will pro - claim your praise. You are good to those who wait for you, to all who seek you.

You shall love the Lord your God

NEIGHBOR

You shall love the Lord your God with all your heart, and with all your soul, and with all your strength, and with all your mind; and your neigh-bor as your-self, your neigh-bor as your-self.

Music: James E. Clemens, 2007. Copyright © 2007 James E. Clemens. All rights reserved. Used by permission.

O God, your word is a lamp

LIGHT

Canon

O God, your word is a lamp to my feet and a

light to my path. The light and peace of

Je - sus Christ be with us. us.

Optional Piano (ad lib)

Jesus said, "I am the bread of life"

BREAD OF LIFE

Music: James E. Clemens, 2007. Copyright © 2007 James E. Clemens. All rights reserved. Used by permission.

Call to intercession

Response following spoken words and petitions:

In your mer - cy, Lord, hear our prayer.

Response following the spoken Benediction

A - men. A - men.

Lord, open our lips

CALL TO PRAISE

Lord, o-pen our lips and our mouths will pro-claim your praise. You are good to those who wait for you, to all who seek you.

You shall love the Lord your God

NEIGHBOR

O God, your word is a lamp

LIGHT

O God, your word is a lamp to my feet and a light to my path. The light and peace of Je-sus Christ be with us.

Music: James E. Clemens, 2007. Copyright © 2007 James E. Clemens. All rights reserved. Used by permission.

Jesus said, "I am the bread of life"

BREAD OF LIFE

Je-sus said, "I am the bread of life. Who-ev-er comes to me will nev-er be hun-gry, and who-ev-er be-lieves in me will nev-er be thirst-y." Lord Je-sus, you have the words of e-ter-nal life.